How Buddhism Began

This book takes a fresh look at the earliest Buddhist texts and offers various suggestions how the teachings in them had developed. Two themes predominate, firstly, it argues that we cannot understand the Buddha unless we understand that he was debating with other religious teachers, notably brahmins. For example, he denied the existence of a "soul"; but what exactly was he denying? Another chapter suggests that the canonical story of the Buddha's encounter with a brigand who wore a garland of his victims' fingers probably reflects an encounter with a form of ecstatic religion.

The other main theme concerns metaphor, allegory and literalism. By taking the words of the texts literally—despite the Buddha's warning not to—successive generations of his disciples created distinctions and developed doctrines far beyond his original intention. One chapter shows how this led to a scholastic categorisation of meditation. Failure to understand a basic metaphor also gave rise to the later argument between the Mahayana and the older tradition. Perhaps most important of all, a combination of literalism with ignorance of the Buddha's allusions to brahminism led Buddhists to forget that the Buddha had preached that love, like Christian charity, could itself be directly salvific.

Richard F. Gombrich was the Boden Professor of Sanskrit at Oxford University. He has written numerous books and articles on Buddhism, in which include *The World of Buddhism: Buddhist Monks and Nuns in Society and Culture* (1991) and *Buddhist Percept and Practise* (1991). He was the President of the Pali Text Society and was honoured with Sri Lanka Ranjana award in 1994 and the SC Chakrabarty medal from the Asiatic Society, Kolkata.

How Buddhism Began

The Conditioned Genesis of the Early Teachings

Richard F. Gombrich

Munshiram Manoharlal
Publishers Pvt. Ltd.

ISBN 978-81-215-0812-4
Reprinted 2002, 2007, 2010, **2014**
First Indian edition 1997

Published with the permission of the Athlone Press, London
This edition for sale in South Asia only

PRINTED IN INDIA
Published by Vikram Jain *for*
Munshiram Manoharlal Publishers Pvt. Ltd.
PO Box 5715, 54 Rani Jhansi Road, New Delhi 110 055, INDIA

www.mrmlbooks.com

For Maria Gerger and Ernst Steinkellner

CONTENTS

CONTENTS

PREFACE

When I was honoured by the invitation to give the Jordan Lectures for 1994, I was also prescribed a format. Four scripts were to be sent in two months in advance, so that they could be photocopied and distributed to anyone willing to buy them. They were to be discussed at seminars, where they would be taken as read. They were to be preceded by a lecture for the general public.

I gave the public lecture at the School of Oriental and African Studies on Monday 14 November. The next two mornings and afternoons were spent in discussing the four circulated papers. Those attending made observations and asked questions; I responded as best I could. At the same time I tried to take notes of what was said and by whom.

My intention was to revise the lectures for publication in the light of the seminar discussions. Most unfortunately, my other duties prevented me from even glancing at the lectures for nine months after they were delivered. On opening the file, I found that my notes, made while trying to think of how to reply, were too sketchy to be of much use. Moreover, some interesting observations had no clear authorship, but my memory could no longer supplement the record. So I must apologise for the scant use I have been able to make of the seminar discussions. A few people kindly wrote to me afterwards, and their contributions are incorporated and acknowledged. I have also made a few other changes to remedy what seemed to me glaring deficiencies. But substantially the five original 'lectures' have not been greatly altered.

It was simple to change the designations of the four pieces which were originally written to be read rather than heard, from 'paper' to 'chapter'. The first, however, was composed as a real lecture, and for a wider audience, so that it had to be in a different style. I have decided to leave it in its original form and reprint it virtually as delivered, only adding some footnotes. I trust that this heterogeneity of presentation, once explained, will not jar on the reader.

I have also decided to be inconsistent in other ways. For example, I am inconsistent in hyphenating Pali, and in whether I quote Pali words in the stem form or the nominative. My only criterion of usage is effectiveness of communication. Thus I am quite deliberately inconsistent in translating many Pali words. Not only do meanings vary with context; it can simply be helpful to see that a Pali word has more than one possible rendition in English. On the other hand, I have of course tried to be consistent where what matters is to realise that the Pali word used is the same. I hope that where the two conflict I have always sacrificed elegance to clarity and that where they do not I have at least a modicum of both.

The terms karma and nirvana I regard as naturalised English words, and I have used them where I am referring to those concepts in general. When I want to refer specifically to the Sanskrit words, e.g. as used in a brahminical context, I use *karman* and *nirvāṇa*; similarly, when I want to refer specifically to uses of the words in the Pali Canon or Theravāda Buddhism I use *kamma* and *nibbāna*. I have taken the liberty of also regarding brahman as a naturalised English word. The stem of this word is the same in Sanskrit and Pali. However, its usage has peculiar problems, because it is often important to differentiate between the neuter form (which refers to the principle) and the masculine form (which refers to a god – or, in the plural, to gods). The latter I call Brahmā, with the plural Brahmās. The hereditary status associated with brahman I refer to by the indigenised English word brahmin.

I am grateful to Kate Crosby and Elizabeth Parsons for skilled secretarial help, a *sine qua non*, and to Lucy Rosenstein for help with the index.

I would also like to record what this book owes to the Numata Foundation, Bukkyo Dendo Kyokai. Their benefaction to Balliol College made it possible to invite Professor Ernst Steinkellner to Oxford, and that in turn led to my visit to his Institute in Vienna where I wrote the whole of chapters 4 and 5, work which I could probably not have done otherwise.

Oxford, September 1995.

ABBREVIATIONS

AA	*Aṅguttara Atthakathā*
AN	*Aṅguttara Nikāya*
AS	*Aṅgulimāla Sutta*
BĀU	*Bṛhad Āraṇyaka Upaniṣad*
ChU	*Chāndogya Upaniṣad*
DA	*Dīgha Atthakathā*
DhA	*Dhammapada Atthakathā*
DN	*Dīgha Nikāya*
D.P.P.N.	*Dictionary of Pāli Proper Names*
J	*Jātaka*
MA	*Majjhima Atthakathā* (=*Ps*)
MN	*Majjhima Nikāya*
Pad	*Paramattha-dīpanī*
P.E.D.	The Pali Text Society's *Pali-English Dictionary*
Ps	*Papañca-sūdanī* (=*MA*)
RV	*Ṛg Veda*
SA	*Saṃyutta Atthakathā*
SN	*Saṃyutta Nikāya*
s.v.	*sub voce*
Thag	*Thera-gāthā*
Ud	*Udāna*
Vin	*Vinaya*

References to Pali texts are to the editions of the Pali Text Society, unless otherwise stated.

I

Debate, Skill in Means, Allegory and Literalism

In these lectures I am more concerned with formulating problems and raising questions than with providing answers. I want to make it clear at the outset that what I am going to say is about work in progress and that many of my conclusions are tentative – though some are more tentative than others. The more I study, the more vividly I become aware of my literally infinite ignorance,[1] and indeed the more I dislike appearing in a role in which I am supposed, at least according to some, to impress by my learning. I only draw consolation from the epistemology of Karl Popper: that knowledge is inevitably provisional, and that progress is most likely to be made by exposing one's ideas to criticism. I hope that these lectures will provoke criticism, preferably of a constructive kind. I shall be happy if I can learn from the discussions in the four seminars which are to be held over the next two days; and particularly happy if my formulations inspire others to undertake research along the lines I propose – for early Buddhism is sorely in need of intelligent research.[2]

Karl Popper has also warned against essentialism. He has shown that knowledge and understanding do not advance through asking for definitions of what things are, but through asking why they occur and how they work.[3] It is always of paramount

[1] That the ignorance of everyone is literally infinite is so indisputable that in a sense it is banal. Nevertheless, it is one of those banalities of which it may be wise to remind students.

[2] Such research would require a knowledge of Pali, but that should be no great obstacle, for Pali is not a difficult language – far easier than Sanskrit, let alone classical Chinese.

[3] Popper, 1960: section 10, especially pp. 28-9 on methodological essentialism. Popper, 1952, vol. II, p. 14: 'the scientific view of the definition "A puppy is a young dog" would be that it is an answer to the question "*What shall we call* a young dog?" rather than an answer to the question "*What is* a puppy?". (Questions like "*What is* life?" or "*What is* gravity?" do not play any rôle in science.) The scientific use of

Continues...

importance to be clear, and for that purpose one may well need to give working definitions – to explain how one is using terms. In the course of justifying one's usage one may of course say or discover something useful, as one may in the course of any piece of reasoning; but providing a definition is not in itself useful. Let me give a pertinent example. Much that has been said and written in the field of comparative religion is, alas, a waste of time, because it has been concerned with a search for 'correct' definitions. To start with, there has been endless argument over the definition of religion itself. The argument is bound to be endless, because the problem is a pseudo-problem and has no 'correct' solution. A certain definition may serve certain purposes, and hence be justified in that context, but there is no reason why others with different purposes should adopt it. For a long time religion was generally defined by western scholars in terms of belief in a god or gods, and that led to argument over whether Buddhism was a religion, an argument which even had some impact on Buddhists. Anthropologists then discovered that most Buddhists do believe in gods, so to that extent the argument may have had some heuristic value. But whether you can deduce from that that Buddhism is a religion is quite another matter.[4] Those coming from a Christian – and in particular a Protestant – cultural background have been far too ready to equate religion with belief or faith, and this has led to severe distortions in their understanding of other religions.

When I wrote my social history of Theravāda Buddhism (Gombrich, 1988b), which concentrated on Buddhist institutions,

definitions ... may be called its *nominalist* interpretation, as opposed to its Aristotelian or *essentialist* interpretation. In modern science, only nominalist definitions occur, that is to say, shorthand symbols or labels are introduced in order to cut a long story short.' Popper, 1974:20: '... essentialism is mistaken in suggesting that definitions can add to our *knowledge of facts....*' In the last-cited passage Popper shows how essentialism involves the false belief 'that there are authoritative sources of our knowledge'.

[4] There are good reasons for calling Buddhism a religion – and it is so called by common consent – but not by virtue of belief in gods.

I thought it prudent to begin with a reasoned defence of the very idea of writing a social history of religion. To some, after all, the notion that the expression of or belief in eternal truths was affected by the contingencies of history might smack of sacrilege. In chapter 3 of that book I showed how some at least of the Buddha's teachings were formulated in response to conditions around him, both social and intellectual; and I am happy to say that my enterprise has not, so far as I am aware, given any offence.

My interest in these lectures is more strictly in doctrinal history, in explicit ideas. My first two seminar papers (chapters 2 and 3) mainly pursue the theme of how the Buddha's teachings emerged through debate with other religious teachers of his day. But both today and in the seminar papers, especially the third (chapter 4), I shall also discuss the next stage in the development of Buddhist doctrine: how his early followers, in attempting to preserve the Buddha's teachings, subtly and unintentionally may have changed them. This immediately raises two questions. 1) How are Buddhists likely to react to the idea that some of what we read in the Pali Canon must have been created by the Buddha's followers? 2) More generally, how do I see the relation between what the Buddha said and the texts which report his words?

I shall offer answers to these two questions very soon. As a background to my answers, however, I must first return to my bugbear, essentialism, and its opposite, nominalism.

The validity of an intellectual position in no way depends on authority; it does not matter who holds it or has held it in the past, though in religious communities, and even, I am afraid, in academia, most people seem to think so. The mere fact that Karl Popper and the Buddha agree about something proves nothing. Nevertheless, as a historian I find it interesting that they broadly agree about essentialism. The brahminical scriptures of the Buddha's day, the Brāhmaṇas and the early Upaniṣads, were mainly concerned with a search for the essences of things: of man, of sacrifice, of the universe. Indeed, brahminical philosophy continued in this essentialist mode down the centuries. The Buddha claimed not to be a philosopher; but the implications of all his teachings were so clearly nominalist that for over a thousand years Buddhist philosophy maintained the tradition that things as we conceive of them and talk about them are mere conceptualisations, mere labels – *prajñapti-mātra*. This has sometimes been interpreted to mean that early Buddhism, like the much later Yogācāra school, was idealistic; but that is a mistake: the ontology of the Pali Canon is realistic and pluralistic; it does not deny that there is a world 'out there'.[5]

In her admirable doctoral thesis, '*The Constitution of the Human Being according to Early Buddhism*' (Hamilton, 1993), Dr Sue Hamilton has shown that the Buddha argued in the non-essentialist way that Popper has shown to characterise science. It is well known that the Buddha divided every sentient being into five sets of components (called *khandha* in Pali): physical form, feelings, apperceptions,[6] volitions and consciousness. Dr Hamilton demonstrates meticulously and convincingly that what interested the Buddha (if we can use that as a shorthand for the authors of the early texts) was how these components functioned; he discussed what they are only to the extent necessary for discussing how they work.

I would also argue that the Buddha took a non-essentialist view of Buddhism itself. Here we must be clear what we mean by 'Buddhism'. The Buddha separated the content of his teachings, the *dharma*, from their institutionalisation, which in the Theravāda tradition came to be called *sāsana*. The *dharma* is a set of truths, and as such is abstract and eternal, like all truths – think for example of the truths of mathematics. The truths exist – are true – whether anyone is aware of them or not. They belong to what Popper calls world three, the world of abstractions.[7]

[5] Whether the Buddha himself had an ontology at all is one of the topics discussed (though by no means exhaustively) in chapter 2.

[6] Apperception is perception which involves recognition. See p. 92.

[7] Introduced as 'the third world' in Popper, 1972. (The 'Preface' to that book refers to the change in terminology.)

Abstractions act causally on the worlds of mental events (Popper's world two) and physical states (Popper's world one) but do not depend on them for their existence.

Similarly, the Buddha rediscovered the eternal truths of the *dharma* and by making them known made them affect the minds and lives of others. Indeed the truths of the *dharma* have a prescriptive force: they point towards release from the round of rebirth, liberation from empirical existence. The Buddha said that just as the ocean has one flavour, that of salt, his teaching had one flavour, that of liberation.[8] (One could indeed say that liberation was the essence of his teaching; but that is not essentialism: it merely describes what his teaching was about.) The Buddha stressed that what gave him the right to preach his doctrine as the truth was that he had *experienced* its truth himself, not just learnt it from others or even just reasoned it out.[9]

Buddhism as a historical phenomenon, I have said, is called the *sāsana*. One of the basic propositions of the *dharma*, of Buddhism as doctrine, is that all empirical phenomena, all mental events and physical states, are impermanent. This applies to the *sāsana*, to Buddhism as an empirical phenomenon, as much as to anything else. The Buddha is even supposed, according to the Pali Canon, to have commented on its incipient decline during his lifetime[10] and, on another occasion, to have predicted its disappearance.[11] Buddhists of all traditions accept that the *sāsana* founded in our world by Gotama Buddha will disappear; but they also believe that the Buddha whom we regard as a historical figure is but one in an infinite series of Buddhas, so that over the vast aeons of time the *dharma* is repeatedly rediscovered and re-promulgated – only in due course to be forgotten again. (It reminds me in a melancholy way of my long career in the

[8] AN IV, 203.

[9] E.g. DN I, 12; the whole of the subsequent passage (in the *Brahmajāla Sutta*) rests on this argument.

[10] MN I, 444-5. For more instances see Rahula, 1956:201-3.

[11] AN IV, 278 = Vin II, 256.

teaching profession.) Buddhists readily accept, therefore, that Buddhism as we can now witness it is in decline; they might even accept such labels as 'corrupt' and 'syncretistic'. They should have no trouble in accepting the proposition on which these lectures are based: that Buddhism as a human phenomenon has no unchanging essence but must have begun to change from the moment of its inception.

This seems, however, to worry some modern scholars. Not long ago I attended a meeting of the British historians of Indian religions at which there was a discussion not, I am glad to say, about the definition of religion, but about the definition of Buddhism. I do not think that most of the participants approached the question in an essentialist spirit: they were ready to accept that Buddhism could be adequately defined, in a nominalist manner, as the religion of those who claim to be Buddhists. But they asked whether the various forms of Buddhism which gave those people their religious identity had any common features. They failed to find any, and reached the rather despairing conclusion that Buddhism was therefore not a useful concept at all.

I think this is to go too far. True, it is not *prima facie* obvious that there are features common to the religions of a traditional Theravādin rice-farmer, a Japanese Pure Land Buddhist, and a member of the UK branch of the Soka Gakkai International. This may not bother the Buddhists themselves, secure within their own traditions, and I am not aware that they have seriously discussed the problem. But I suggest that the Buddha's teaching again offers a solution – through the doctrine of causation, conditioned genesis. For the Buddha and his followers, things – they focused mainly on living beings – exist not as adamantine essences but as dynamic processes. These processes are not random (*adhicca-samuppanna*) but causally determined. Any empirical phenomenon is seen as a causal sequence, and that applies to the *sāsana* too. 'One thing leads to another,' as the English idiom has it. Whether or not we can see features common to the religion of Mr Richard Causton, the late leader of the UK branch of Soka

Gakkai International,[12] and that of Nāgārjuna, or of the Buddha himself, there is a train of human events which causally connects them. Buddhism is not an inert object: it is a chain of events.

In these lectures I want to apply this Buddhist insight to Buddhism's own history, and mainly to an area in which too little historical work has been done: the earliest texts. I am not making the absurd claim that I am breaking new ground by saying that Buddhism has a history. But the obvious sometimes needs restating and the frontiers of knowledge prevented from contracting. That extreme form of relativism which claims that one reading of a text, for instance of a historical document, is as valid as another, I regard as such a contraction of knowledge. I wish to take a Buddhist middle way between two extremes. One extreme is the deadly over-simplification which is inevitable for beginners but out of place in a university, the over-simplification which says that 'The Buddha taught X' or 'Mahāyānists believe Y', without further qualification. The other extreme is the deconstruction fashionable among social scientists who refuse all generalisation, ignore the possibilities of reasonable extrapolation, and usually leave us unenlightened (Gombrich, 1992b:159).[13] I hope not just to preach against these extremes but to show by example where the middle way lies.

* * *

[12] Causton, 1988. See also Wilson & Dobbelaere, 1994, especially the 'Introduction'.

[13] See also the words of my distinguished predecessor as Jordan Lecturer, Professor David Seyfort Ruegg: 'In Buddhist hermeneutics as traditionally practised, there can be no question of radically relativizing the intended purport of a canonical utterance or text (so-called semantic autonomy) and banishing the idea of authorial intention (so-called authorial irrelevance) in favour of an interpretation, or "reading", gained against the background of the reader's (or listener's) prejudgement or preknowledge. Buddhist hermeneutical theory, although it most certainly takes into account the pragmatic situation and the performative and perlocutionary aspects of linguistic communication, differs accordingly from much contemporary writing on the subject of literary interpretation and the hermeneutic circle.' (Ruegg, 1989:31-2, fn. 40.) For my own (Popperian) understanding of the 'hermeneutic circle', see Gombrich, 1993b, sections IV and V.

I have applied the Buddhist teachings of impermanence and conditioned genesis to Buddhist history as a whole. Let me now apply them to the main subject matter of my inquiry, the texts of the Pali Canon. What kind of entity are these texts?

In other fields of learning it is commonplace that during the course of transmission over many centuries texts are subject to corruption and it is a primary duty of scholars to analyse, and if possible to repair, that corruption. The critical study of the text of the Bible got under way in the nineteenth century and is accepted nowadays as being fundamental to the serious study of Christianity. Though many would assent in the abstract to the proposition that Buddhist texts should be studied in the same way, that assent has so far had surprisingly little impact on the study of the Pali Canon. This may be due more to a dearth of competent scholars than to any theoretical objections. The Pali commentaries on the Canon which were put into the form in which we have them by Buddhaghosa and others in Sri Lanka and South India,[14] probably in the fifth and sixth centuries A.D.,[15] sometimes discuss variant readings in the texts, so the spotting of ancient corruptions is nothing alien to the Theravādin tradition.

Modern editors of the Pali Canon, however, have generally contented themselves with trying to establish a *textus receptus* or 'received text'. Let me explain. Most of our physical evidence for the Pali Canon is astonishingly recent, far more recent than our physical evidence for the western classical and biblical texts. While talking of this, I want to take the opportunity to correct a mistake in something I published earlier this year. In Professor K. R. Norman's splendid revision of Geiger's *Pali Grammar*, published by the Pali Text Society (Geiger, 1994), I wrote an introduction called 'What is Pali?' (Gombrich, 1994a). In that I wrote (p. xxv) that a Kathmandu manuscript of c.800 A.D. is 'the

[14] Norman 1983:134 : Dhammapāla lived in South India and probably visited Anuradhapura.

[15] K. R. Norman, *ibid.*, section III.3, pp. 118-37.

oldest substantial piece of written Pali to survive' if we except the inscriptions from Devnimori and Ratnagiri, which differ somewhat in phonetics from standard Pali. This is wrong. One can quibble about what 'substantial' means; but it must surely include a set of twenty gold leaves found in the Khin Ba Gôn trove near Śrī Kṣetra, Burma, by Duroiselle in 1926-7. The leaves are inscribed with eight excerpts from the Pali Canon. Professor Harry Falk has now dated them, on paleographic grounds, to the second half of the fifth century A.D., which makes them by far the earliest physical evidence for the Pali canonical texts (Stargardt, 1995).

I am glad to make this correction. However, the survival of a few short extracts is not important for the overall picture I am trying to present. The gross fact remains that almost all our evidence for the texts of the Buddhist Canon comes from manuscripts and that hardly any Pali manuscripts are more than about five hundred years old. The vast majority are less than three hundred years old.

That does not mean that we have no older evidence for readings. The commentaries, even though they too are available to us in similarly recent manuscripts, provide many opportunities for cross-checking. They may occasionally have been tampered with, but in general where a commentary confirms a reading in the canonical text we can assume that we have access to what the commentator read in the fifth or sixth century. However, the commentators only quote or comment on a minority of the words in the texts.

By comparing Pali manuscripts from Sri Lanka, Burma, Thailand and Cambodia modern editors have tried to get back to what those early commentators read: that is what I mean by the *textus receptus*. But those commentators lived eight or nine centuries after the Buddha and about half a millennium after the time, in the first century B.C., when (according to a plausible tradition) the Canon was first committed to writing. The canonical texts cannot be later than the first century B.C., and in fact I would argue that most of them must go back in substance to at least the third century B.C.. During centuries of transmission both oral and written they were inevitably subject to corruption. And I think that anyone who reads the texts while keeping this simple fact in mind rapidly becomes aware that plenty of passages do indeed appear to be corrupt.

What is one to do? Let me, for simplicity, consider just the sermons, the *suttas*. Most of them survive also in Chinese translation, sometimes in more than one version. A great deal can be gained by comparing the Pali with the Chinese versions. I unfortunately know no Chinese and am dependent on the help of others. But in my third seminar paper (chapter 4) I hope to show by example how useful recourse to the Chinese version of a *sutta* can be.

Nevertheless, this line of approach faces great difficulties. The initial obstacle, of course, is that the number of people in the world with the necessary knowledge of Chinese and Pali is probably in single figures, and even they have to spend most of their time on other things in order to make a living. Since Chinese is certainly the harder language of the two, I put my faith for the future in the scholarship of the Far East, where many students come to university already knowing classical Chinese. The study of Theravāda has not so far flourished in countries with a Mahāyāna tradition, but there are hopeful signs that that is beginning to change.

A different kind of problem lies in the limitations of the material. Very few Chinese translations of the texts found in the Pali canon were made before the last quarter of the fourth century A.D. (Zürcher, 1959:202-4). The translations were not made from the Pali but from different recensions in other Indian languages. All translators make mistakes, and these translators cannot have been exceptions. And not all of them, perhaps, shared our ideas about literal accuracy. But since the versions they were translating from are now lost, we can only guess at the accuracy of the translations.

However, there is something we can do with the Pali texts even without comparing them with the Chinese versions. We can apply our critical intelligence, and at least point out where the texts seem to be incoherent and may therefore be corrupt. Occasionally, we may even be able to suggest an emendation. Editors have hitherto been reluctant to suggest any emendation which has no manuscript support. I would like them to be bolder. Provided always that one states in a footnote what the manuscripts read, I can see no harm in printing as text what would make better sense. Even if the suggested emendation finds no acceptance, what has been lost? But surely some emendations will be convincing. In my final seminar paper (chapter 5) I shall show how the change of a single letter can make a garbled text meaningful, and I feel confident that here at least an emendation which has no manuscript support will be accepted as probable, if not even certain.

What, then, do I think of the relation between these texts and what the Buddha taught? It seems that I have in the past been guilty of giving a misleading impression of where I stand on this issue, so I had better try to redress the balance. At the Seventh World Sanskrit Conference, held in Leiden in 1987, Professor Lambert Schmithausen kindly invited me to contribute to a panel (which in Holland it is now politically correct to call a 'workshop') entitled 'The Earliest Buddhism'. When the proceedings of that panel were published (Ruegg & Schmithausen, 1990), Professor Schmithausen, certainly with the best intentions, gave a summary of my position which I do not accept; he painted me into a kind of fundamentalist corner. This arose, no doubt, because in my paper (Gombrich, 1990) I argued that some of the arguments that have been put forward to show that certain ideas found in the Pali Canon must post-date the Buddha were invalid, and that inconsistencies in the texts did not themselves prove their inauthenticity. For example, I argued that a sacred tradition is at least as likely to iron out inconsistencies as to introduce them; this is what textual critics know as the principle of *lectior difficilior potior*, that the banal reading is more likely to replace the oddity than *vice versa.*[16] I am afraid I poked some fun at work done by Professor Schmithausen and others on textual accounts of achieving Enlightenment; I found their analyses excessively literal-minded, and argued that the same person – even the Buddha – might on different occasions give different accounts of such ineffable experiences. The one point at which I did argue positively that certain things in the texts must go back to the Buddha himself was when I pointed out that they were jokes, and asked rhetorically, 'Are jokes ever composed by committees?' The positive part of my paper, however, was mainly devoted to showing that the texts contained important allusions to brahminism of which the commentators were unaware. This proves that 'the earliest Buddhism' has interesting features which we can uncover but which the later Buddhist tradition had forgotten about; it does not prove that those features must go back to the Buddha himself, though I do think that in some cases the evidence is suggestive. But I do not, in Professor Schmithausen's words, 'take divergencies within these materials' (the Nikāyas), 'and even incoherences ... to be of little significance'; still less do I 'regard doctrinal developments during the oral period of transmission to have been minimal' (p. 1). However, rather than argue over a description of my position, which would be an essentialist fatuity, I have tried to illustrate it in the four seminar papers (chapters 2 to 5) by a series of concrete examples. I should say however, that my main purpose is not to stratify the texts, even if that is a by-product of some of my arguments. I want to trace the evolution of some of the ideas contained in the Buddha's teachings as reported in the Pali texts, in order to get a clearer idea of what the texts are saying.

* * *

[16] Let me here note in passing that levelling has also occurred in the Canon on a vast scale as passages were transferred from their original contexts to be repeated in other contexts.

Let me now turn, for the rest of this lecture, to outlining the processes and mechanisms of that evolution which I shall be discussing in more detail in the seminars. The first of these is debate. In my publications over the last few years I have repeatedly stressed that the Buddha, like anyone else, was communicating in a social context, reacting to his social environment and hoping in turn to influence those around him. The Buddha's experience of Enlightenment was of course private and beyond language, but the truth or truths to which he had 'awakened' had to be expressed in language, which is irreducibly social. I am not referring so much to language in the narrow literal sense, like Sanskrit or Pali, but to the set of categories and concepts which that language embodies. The *dharma* is the product of argument and debate, the debate going on in the oral culture of renouncers and brahmins (*samaṇa-brāhmaṇa*), as the recurrent phrase has it, in the upper Ganges plain in the fifth century B.C..

I have to stress, unfortunately, that our evidence for that environment is sadly deficient. The recent book by Professor Harry Falk (Falk, 1993) should finally lay to rest any notion that writing may have existed in India in the Buddha's day: there is no firm evidence for it until the reign of Asoka, one and a half centuries later. The brahmin texts to which the Buddha was reacting may well have changed since his day. Since they were orally preserved, he was quoting, or perhaps I should rather say alluding to them, from memory. Moreover, they were somewhat esoteric, so that as a non-brahmin he may not have had easy access to them. Matters are worse with the groups of renouncers. The texts of the Canon do refer explicitly to some doctrines of the Jains and of several other heterodox (i.e., non-Vedic) groups, but these allusions to opponents' arguments could well be distorted. The Jain texts that have come down to us were probably first written down in the fifth century A.D.; some of the material is certainly very much older, but scientific study of the voluminous and very difficult Jain texts is in its infancy. However, what we do have is enough to show that some (not all) of the teaching ascribed by the Buddhist texts to Mahāvīra, a younger contemporary of the Buddha's, is quite unlike what Jain tradition holds him to have taught. The other heterodox sects are even worse off than the Jains, for none of their own texts have survived. All this means that we are sure to miss many – innumerable – allusions, and not even to know what we are missing.

That is gloomy; but we can cheer up a bit when we recall that we have after all recovered some allusions which had so far been missed by both ancient and modern commentators. We have now found, for example, several allusions to the Upaniṣads; but as recently as 1927 no less a scholar than Louis de La Vallée Poussin was able to write that he believed that the Upaniṣads were not known to the Buddhists (de la Vallée Poussin 1927:12).

If, as I argue, the *dharma* emerged from debate, that has two consequences that I wish to explore. One relates to consistency, the other to comparative study. Let me explore the latter first. In doing so, I hope to be fulfilling a part of my brief; for the Jordan lectures are explicitly in *comparative* religion.

To see the genesis of the Buddha's teaching as conditioned by the religious milieu in which it arose is to adopt a truly Buddhist viewpoint which I also believe to be good historiography. It is also to take a middle way between the view that Buddhism is just a form of Hinduism and the view that it owes nothing to its Indian background. To put the matter so starkly may sound absurd, and I may seem to be forcing an open door. But in fact I think that ninety-nine per cent of the teaching about Buddhism which takes place in the world goes to one or the other of those extremes. Let me try to justify this pessimistic claim.

There has been a strong trend in the Indian sub-continent to over-emphasise the Buddha's Hindu background. Hindu polemicists in the first millennium A.D. claimed, indeed, that the Buddha was just an incarnation of Viṣṇu (Gupta, 1991). Some said that in taking this form Viṣṇu's aim was to mislead the gullible and weed out those who were not true Vaiṣṇavas;[17] others at least considered the Buddha benign because of his preaching against animal sacrifice.[18] A modern version of this attempt to colonise Buddhism is the official government view in Nepal, that Buddhism is merely a branch of Hinduism. This means that it need not figure in the school syllabus:[19] Hinduism is taught, but there is no requirement to teach the 'Buddhist' part of it, and if Buddhists complain, they can be told that their religion, Hinduism, is indeed taught. When I have lectured on Buddhism in Indian universities I have found the view that the Buddha was 'born a Hindu' and was a Hindu reformer to be virtually universal. That the very idea of 'Hinduism' at that period is wildly anachronistic is a subtlety that seems to bother no one.

The other extreme may be politically more innocent, but intellectually it is probably even more misleading. To present the Buddha's teaching without explaining its Indian background must be to miss many of its main points. Let me give a simple, yet crucial, example. In western languages, the Buddha is presented as having taught the doctrine (*vāda*) of 'no soul' (*anātman*). What is being denied – what is a soul? Western languages are at home in the Christian cultural tradition. Christian theologians have differed vastly over what the soul is. For Aristotle, and thus for Aquinas, it is the form of the body, what makes a given individual person a whole rather than a mere assemblage of parts. However, most Christians conceive of the soul, however vaguely, in a completely different way, which goes back to Plato: that the soul is precisely other than the body, as in the common expression 'body and soul', and is some kind of disembodied mental, and above all, moral, agent, which survives the body at death. But none of this has anything to do with the Buddha's position. He was opposing the Upaniṣadic theory of the soul. In

[17] E.g. *Viṣṇu Purāṇa* 3, 17, 42; *Bhāgavata Purāṇa* 1, 3, 24.
[18] E.g. *Pauṣkara Saṃhitā* 36, 226.
[19] Dr David N. Gellner, personal communication.

the Upaniṣads the soul, *ātman*, is opposed to both the body and the mind; for example, it cannot exercise such mental functions as memory or volition. It is an essence, and by definition an essence does not change. Furthermore, the essence of the individual living being was claimed to be literally the same as the essence of the universe. This is not a complete account of the Upanisadic soul, but adequate for present purposes.

Once we see what the Buddha was arguing against, we realise that it was something very few westerners have ever believed in and most have never even heard of. He was refusing to accept that a person had an unchanging essence. Moreover, since he was interested in how rather than what, he was not so much saying that people are made of such and such components, and the soul is not among them, as that people function in such and such ways, and to explain their functioning there is no need to posit a soul. The approach is pragmatic, not purely theoretical. Of course the Buddha claims that his pragmatism will work because it is based on correct assumptions, so people are bound sooner or later to discuss those assumptions and thus will easily slip back into theorising and into ontology. This, I think, explains why on the one hand there are Pali texts, such as the *Anatta-lakkhaṇa Sutta,*[20] which can reasonably be interpreted to deny the soul, while on the other hand the Buddha seems to avoid putting forward a 'theory' (*vāda*) of his own: he says, for example, that an enlightened monk neither agrees nor disagrees with anyone but goes along with what is being said in the world without being attached to it (MN I, 500). Similarly, he says that he does not dispute with the world; it is the world that disputes with him (SN III,138). It seems but a short step from here to the statement that he has no viewpoint (*diṭṭhi*) at all; but this extreme position is found only, I believe, in one group of poems.[21] A proselytising

[20] Vin I,13.

[21] The *Aṭṭhaka* and *Pārāyaṇa Vagga*s of the *Sutta-nipāta*; see e.g. verses 787, 800, 882. I shall return to this point at the beginning of chapter 2 below.

religion cannot dispense with discussion, and many texts do show the Buddha debating. While the evidence is thus somewhat inconsistent, on balance one may conclude that the Buddha was against discussing theory in the abstract, that he did not pick arguments, and that when discussion arose he avoided head-on confrontation by adopting 'skill in means'.

* * *

The Buddha's 'skill in means' tends to be thought of as a feature of the Mahāyāna. It is true that the term translated 'skill in means', *upāya-kauśalya*, is post-canonical, but the exercise of skill to which it refers, the ability to adapt one's message to the audience, is of enormous importance in the Pali Canon. T.W. Rhys Davids wrote about it nearly a century ago, in 1899, in his book *Dialogues of the Buddha, part 1*, which is a translation of the first third of the *Dīgha Nikāya*. Since I could not improve on them, I shall quote his words at some length.

'When speaking on sacrifice to a sacrificial priest, on union with God to an adherent of the current theology, on Brahman claims to superior social rank to a proud Brahman, on mystic insight to a man who trusts in it, on the soul to one who believes in the soul theory, the method followed is always the same. Gotama puts himself as far as possible in the mental position of the questioner. He attacks none of his cherished convictions. He accepts as the starting-point of his own exposition the desirability of the act or condition prized by his opponent – of the union with God (as in the *Tevijja*), or of sacrifice (as in the *Kūṭadanta*), or of social rank (as in the *Ambaṭṭha*), or of seeing heavenly sights, etc. (as in the *Mahāli*), or of the soul theory (as in the *Poṭṭhapāda*). He even adopts the very phraseology of his questioner. And then, partly by putting a new and (from the Buddhist point of view) a higher meaning into the words; partly by an appeal to such ethical conceptions as are common ground between them; he gradually leads his opponent up to his conclusion. This is, of course, always Arahatship....

There is both courtesy and dignity in the method employed. But no little dialectic skill, and an easy mastery of the ethical points involved, are required to bring about the result....
On the hypothesis that he was an historical person, of that training and character he is represented in the Piṭakas to have had, the method is precisely that which it is most probable he would have actually followed.
Whoever put the Dialogues together may have had a sufficiently clear memory of the way he conversed, may well have even remembered particular occasions and persons. To the mental vision of the compiler, the doctrine taught loomed so much larger than anything else, that he was necessarily more concerned with that, than with any historical accuracy in the details of the story. He was, in this respect, in much the same position as Plato when recording the dialogues of Socrates. But he was not, like Plato, giving his own opinions. We ought, no doubt, to think of compilers rather than of a compiler. The memory of co-disciples had to be respected, and kept in mind. And so far as the actual doctrine is concerned our dialogues are probably a more exact representation of the thoughts of the teacher than the dialogues of Plato.
However this may be, the method followed in all these dialogues has one disadvantage. In accepting the position of the adversary, and adopting his language, the authors compel us, in order to follow what they give us as Gotama's view, to read a good deal between the lines. The *argumentum ad hominem* can never be the same as a statement of opinion given without reference to any particular person.'[22]

If the Buddha was continually arguing *ad hominem* and adapting what he said to the language of his interlocutor, this must have had enormous implications for the consistency, or rather the inconsistency, of his mode of expression. He had had a clear and compelling vision of the truth and was trying to convey it to a wide range of people with different inclinations and varying presuppositions, so he had to express this message in many different ways. As I have already argued in referring to the

[22] 'Introduction to the Kassapa-Sihanāda Sutta' (Rhys Davids, 1899:206-7). I have modernised the transliteration.

principle of *lectio difficilior potior*, it is logical to expect that the tradition levelled out many of the inconsistencies of expression. If we had a true record of the Buddha's words, I think we would find that during his preaching career of forty-five years he had expressed himself in an enormous number of different ways.

Besides, there is another factor which is easily forgotten. Often the Buddha's preaching was successful in making converts. By the same token converts came from a variety of backgrounds. At that time Buddhism had only rudimentary institutions, no schools and probably rather haphazard socialisation of converts. So many members of the Sangha must have gone on using some of their former terms and concepts,[23] and the Buddha may well have gone on meeting them half way when he talked to them. Thus the variety of expression which characterised the Buddha's skill in means did not stop at conversion, or necessarily die out when the Buddha died, but must have gone on influencing formulations of the teachings. This variety in the backgrounds of the Buddha's disciples means that change within texts they (corporately) composed is unlikely to have been unilinear: several currents must have intermingled.

Debate of course took place within the Sangha as well as around it; and the point I have just made about converts means that a line between the two is hard to draw. Many *suttas* begin with a discussion between two or more monks on a point of doctrine; usually they then go on to the Buddha and ask him to

[23] In Gombrich, 1994b:1079 I have given clear instances of this being done by Buddhist converts from Jainism. There were many more brahmin converts, and they were presumably familiar, at least to some degree, with brahminical ideas and terminology. I thus agree with Professor Bronkhorst that what he calls 'outside influences' account for discrepancies in the texts. However, this lecture should show why I disagree with his claim (made in a rejoinder to Gombrich, 1994b which he has kindly shown me in advance of publication) that all the discrepancies are best explained by a single cause. In explaining a physical phenomenon, such as a chemical reaction, we do try to find a unique set of conditions which triggers it; but social phenomena, including the composition of religious texts, are rarely amenable to a single explanation, and in fact are very often over-determined.

settle the matter, and he may say that they are all right, or that one of them is right, or that all of them are barking up the wrong tree. Such discussions among his followers must have begun from the day the Buddha made his first converts, and no doubt many of the arguments remained unresolved, either because during his lifetime they never reached him or because after his death he was no longer there to arbitrate. In my third seminar paper (chapter 4) I shall give extended examples of such debates, and show how they led to doctrinal developments which must, I believe, postdate the Buddha's death, though they appear in sermons ascribed to him.

The Buddha's arguments with proponents of other views were sometimes allegorised. Take, for example, the beginning of the *Mahāvagga* of the *Vinaya Piṭaka*. This section of text, which is essentially the narrative of how the Buddha came to found the Sangha, was immensely famous and also circulated as a separate text under the Sanskrit name of the *Catuṣ-pariṣat-sūtra*, the *sūtra* of the four assemblies. The text begins at the point when the Buddha has just attained Enlightenment. This attainment is expressed in a set of three verses (Vin I, 2) in which he repeatedly refers to himself as a brahmin. The Buddha was not a brahmin in the literal sense, i.e. born as one, but the *Sutta Piṭaka* contains several passages in which he argues that brahmin, properly understood, is not a social character but a moral one, referring to a person who is wise and virtuous. In the *Mahāvagga* a snooty brahmin then comes along and asks him by virtue of what he can claim to be a brahmin. The Buddha answers in a verse, his fourth, which includes puns on brahminical terms, one of them a pun on the word *brāhmaṇa* (in a Prakritic form[24]). This is the usual kind of display of 'skill in means', twisting his opponent's terminology. Shortly thereafter,

[24] The Prakritic form (which I presume stood where *brāhmaṇo* now stands at Vin I p. 3, line 5) was *bāhaṇo*, which is ironically etymologised as one who has 'expelled' (*bāhita-*) evil teachings.

however, the Buddha is on the point of deciding that to preach what he had discovered would be too much trouble. At this, Brahmā appears, kneels before the Buddha with a suppliant gesture, and begs him to preach. The Buddha makes Brahmā ask three times before he accedes to the request.

Brahmā is the highest god of the brahmins, and more; he is also the personification of the principle, *brahman*, which on the one hand makes a brahmin a brahmin and on the other hand is disclosed by brahmin mysticism as the only true reality. So here the epitome of all that brahmins hold sacred is presented, in personified form, as humbling himself before the Buddha, declaring that the Buddha has opened the door to immortality (which brahmins had claimed to lie in or through Brahman), and begging him to reveal the truth to the world.This text continues to make extensive use of allegory, notably in the long story leading up to the Buddha's delivery of what is known as the Fire Sermon,[25] in which he preaches that all our senses and their operations, including the operations of consciousness, are on fire with passion, hatred and delusion. I must postpone this and other instances of allegory until my second seminar paper (chapter 3).

* * *

Whether the Buddha himself used allegory I am not sure; it may be part of the skill in means of the compilers of the texts. Allegory, which I take to be the extension of metaphor into a narrative, is an artful form of literalism. I would also argue, on the other hand, that unintentional literalism has been a major force for change in the early doctrinal history of Buddhism. Texts have been interpreted with too much attention to the precise words used and not enough to the speaker's intention, the spirit of the text. In particular I see in some doctrinal developments what I call scholastic literalism, which is a tendency to take the words

[25] Vin I, 34-5.

and phrases of earlier texts (maybe the Buddha's own words) in such a way as to read in distinctions which it was never intended to make. I shall have a good deal to say about this in the seminar papers.

The Buddha seems to have had a lively awareness of the dangers of literalism. A short text, AN II, 135, classifies people who hear his teachings into four types; the terms are explained at *Puggala-paññatti* IV, 5 (= p. 41). As commonly, the list is hierarchic, the best type being listed first. The first type (*ugghaṭita-ññu*) understands the teaching as soon as it is uttered; the second (*vipacita-ññu*) understands on mature reflection;[26] the third (*neyya*) is 'leadable': he understands it when he has worked at it, thought about it and cultivated wise friends. The fourth is called *pada-parama*, 'putting the words first'; he is defined as one who though he hears much, preaches much, remembers much and recites much does not come within this life to understand the teaching. One could hardly ask for a clearer condemnation of literalism. As throughout this lecture, I am merely pointing out that Buddhism provides the best tools for its own exegesis.

In fact there is an extremely famous text in the Pali Canon in which the Buddha criticises literalism. But I see a great irony here, for the words of the text have been too literally interpreted, so that its point has been missed. I am referring to the simile of the raft in the *Alagaddūpama Sutta* (MN *sutta* 22), the sermon with the simile of the water snake.

This text begins with the wicked obstinacy of a monk called Ariṭṭha. He persists in saying, 'My understanding of the Buddha's teaching is that if one practises the things the Buddha declared to be obstacles, they are no obstacles.' Of course, he cannot have said exactly that, for it is self-contradictory. The

[26] I follow the reading at AN II, 135 and give it my own interpretation. *Puggala-paññatti* 41 reads *vipaccita*; the commentary on the latter also reads *vipaccita*, but with a variant *vipañcita*, and glosses it as *vitthārita*, so that the second type becomes one who understands the teaching when it has been expanded. This latter interpretation is also that of Ruegg (1989:187), following other post-canonical sources which read *vipañcita*.

things 'declared to be obstacles' is a euphemism for sexual intercourse; Ariṭṭha is criticising the first rule in the monastic code, that prohibiting sexual intercourse. The monks report Ariṭṭha to the Buddha, who reprimands him in the strongest terms and says he has not got so much as a whiff of the doctrine and discipline. The Buddha rehearses with the monks that he has compared sensual desire to all kinds of dangerous and unpleasant things, and points out that one cannot have sexual intercourse without sensual desire (p. 133). From this I deduce that Ariṭṭha had maintained that the Buddha may have preached against sensual desire but that he did not preclude sexual intercourse.

The Buddha then goes on to say that some foolish people memorise his teachings but do not use their intelligence to work out what they mean, so that the teachings afford them no insight. The advantages they derive from their learning are being able to criticise others and to quote; but they do not get what should be the real benefit of such learning. Because they have misunderstood the teaching, it only does them harm. He compares this to catching hold of a water snake. The simile rests on the fact that 'misunderstood' in Pali, *duggahīta*, literally means 'badly grasped'. A man who hunts a water snake and when he finds it grasps it by the coils or tail gets bitten and may even die, because he has grasped it badly. Conversely (p. 134), someone who has properly grasped his teachings, says the Buddha, will derive benefit from them, like a man who holds the snake down with a cleft stick and then grasps it by the neck. 'So,' the Buddha concludes, 'if you understand the meaning of something I say, remember it; if you don't understand it, ask me or one of the wise monks' (p. 134).

These words are immediately followed by the famous simile of the raft. The Buddha compares his teaching to a raft. A man might come to a large body of water with no visible means of getting across, and build himself a raft. Once across, he would not need to carry that raft with him but would, if he were sensible, abandon it. 'Even so,' says the Buddha, 'I have taught my teachings to be like a raft, for the sake of crossing over, not for holding on to. If, monks, you understand them to be like a raft, you will let go of my teachings, let alone of things I have not taught.'

This last sentence has been interpreted – misinterpreted – in many different ways. The problem lies with the word *dhammā*, here in the plural. It is notorious that *dhamma* has many meanings and is often hard to translate. But I think the meaning of the raft simile is perfectly clear from the context.

In the previous passage, which I have summarised, the Buddha refers to his teaching sometimes as *dhamma* in the singular and sometimes as *dhammā* in the plural, just as we in English can talk of his teaching or his teachings without any change in meaning. Similarly, the raft simile happens to begin with *dhamma* in the singular – 'I shall teach you that my teaching is like a raft' – and to end with *dhammā* in the plural; but to imagine that there is a change of reference is sheer scholastic literalism.

The Buddha concludes that his *dhammā*, his teachings, are to be let go of, let alone *adhammā*, non-teachings. The occasion for this whole discourse is given by Ariṭṭha, who obstinately declared that he understood the Buddha's teaching in a certain sense. The Buddha repudiated Ariṭṭha's interpretation of his words with an attack on clinging to the words rather than the spirit. In effect the Buddha said, 'Whatever precise words of mine Ariṭṭha may be quoting, he has missed what I meant.' So when he concludes the raft simile by saying that one should not cling to his teachings, the emphasis is on not clinging to the words of his teachings. The point is not that the content of his teaching is to be abandoned once one is Enlightened, but that his teaching is pragmatic, a means to an end, and that one should not cling to a particular formulation he used – let alone to something he never said at all.[27]

[27] My interpretation differs from that of the great commentator Buddhaghosa (*Papañca-sūdanī* II, 109), but this does not deter me. We must distinguish between meaning and reference – both *attha* in Pali.

Continues...

By taking this text phrase by phrase rather than as a coherent whole, later exegetes have made a strange hash of it. *Dhammā* in the plural can also mean the objects of thought, 'noeta', which correspond to the faculty of thought as sounds correspond to hearing.[28] Lifting the last words out of context, Mahāyāna texts claimed that the Buddha prescribed the abandonment of all objects of thought; and by the same token that he also recommended the abandonment of the opposite, non-objects of thought – whatever they might be.[29] Thus the raft simile became a charter for paradox and irrationality.

Buddhaghosa is right in saying, at the end of his interpretation (bottom of the page), that the last sentence (about leaving *dhammā*, let alone *adhammā*) is aimed at Ariṭṭha. He is taking the passage in context, and says that *adhammā refers* to what Ariṭṭha has been saying. With this I agree. Nevertheless, I think that Buddhaghosa has selected the wrong *meaning* for *adhammā* in this passage.

Clearly *dhammā* and *adhammā* in the sentence are a pair: *adhammā* is the contrary of *dhammā*. *Dhamma* can mean 'prescribed behaviour or condition', and *adhamma* the opposite, a behaviour or condition condemned by the Buddha. Buddhaghosa has selected this meaning of *adhamma* here, but as a result he has to interpret *dhamma* as a recommended state, and to do this he has to find recommended states to which it could refer. He therefore drags in types of meditation, which are mentioned nowhere in the text and are completely alien to the context.

While Buddhaghosa's interpretation of *adhamma* does fit the general context, it goes back to the earlier part of the text and ignores the passage immediately leading up to the raft simile. That passage is about the wrong and the right way to take teachings (*dhammā*), which it compares with the wrong and right way to take hold of a water-snake – hence the name of the *sutta*. In both cases, the verb for 'take' is *gah*. The wrong way is to learn the words of the teachings without understanding their meaning. Teachings thus wrongly taken will only harm the taker, 'because he has taken hold of them wrongly' (*duggahītattā dhammānaṃ* (p. 133)). To take hold of them correctly is to understand their meaning (*attha*), and if so taken they will be beneficial.

[28] See p. 35 below for my hypothesis how the word came to have this meaning.

[29] *Vajracchedikā Prajñāpāramitā*, ed. and tr. Edward Conze, Serie Orientale Roma XIII (Rome, 1957). 'Nor does there take place in these Bodhi-beings, these great beings, a perception of a dharma, and likewise [there is] no perception of a no-dharma. Nor Subhuti, does a perception or no-perception take place in them. And why? If, Subhuti, in these Bodhi-beings, these great beings, a perception of a dharma could take place, that would be with them a seizing on a self, seizing on a being, seizing on a soul, seizing on a person. And why? Because the Bodhi-being, the great being, should not seize upon a dharma or a no-dharma. Therefore this saying has been taught by the Tathagata with a

Continues...

* * *

The Buddha was the great communicator, the supreme master of skill in means, and yet he correctly foresaw that even he would not be able to preserve his teaching from corruption. When he taught, he could at least engage his auditors in dialogue and so make sure that he was, as we would now put it, on their wavelength. I can have no such pretensions to skill in means, and I do not even have the advantage of knowing what the members of my audience presuppose and expect. I only hope that I have been able to convey what I intended.

hidden meaning, 'By those who know the discourse on dharma like unto a raft, dharmas should be forsaken, much more so no-dharmas'.

The Lord: What do you think, Subhuti, is there any dharma which has been fully known by the Tathagata as 'the utmost, right and perfect enlightenment', or is there any dharma which has been demonstrated by the Tathagata?

Subhuti: No, as I understand the Lord's teaching, there is not any dharma which has been fully known by the Tathagata as 'the utmost, right and perfect enlightenment', and there is no dharma which has been demonstrated by the Tathagata. And why? This dharma which has been fully known or demonstrated by the Tathagata, – it is not to be seized, it is not to be talked about, it is neither dharma nor no-dharma.'

The corresponding Sanskrit text is on pp. 31-3.

II

How, not What: *Kamma* as a Ṛeaction to Brahminism

In my first chapter I have said that the Buddha's teaching evolved in dialogue with other religious teachers of his day, especially brahmins; and I have said that he was not an essentialist, and in contrast to brahmins was interested in how things worked rather than in what they were. In this chapter I want to explore both themes further, and to combine them. Towards the end of the chapter I shall work in a third theme, the Buddha's advocacy of kindness, and hope thus to weave a three stranded argument.

One thing about which I feel rather uncertain is how interested the Buddha himself was in presenting a philosophically coherent doctrine. I have no doubt that such a doctrine is to be found in the Pali Canon; but to what extent is it due to later systematisers? Even if it is not due to later hands – and I incline to the unsurprising view that the Buddha was probably a greater thinker, indeed a greater philosopher, than his disciples – are we misrepresenting him if we attribute to him an impressive edifice of argument?

This problem repeated itself later in the history of Buddhist thought. The Mādhyamikas, followers of Nāgārjuna, divided into two camps. On the one side were the Prāsaṅgikas, who held that their philosophy could only serve to demolish the positions held by others. They took as their authority the Buddha's statement that he himself had no viewpoint (*diṭṭhi*),[1] and rigorously avoided trying to establish any position of their own. On the other side the Svātantrikas could appeal for authority to the many canonical passages where the Buddhist right view (*sammā-diṭṭhi*) is contrasted to wrong view (*micchā-diṭṭhi*) and recommended; they set forth positive arguments to show that Buddhism, as interpreted by Nāgārjuna, was both coherent and true.

If we look at the canonical material there is a good deal of evidence on both sides. There can be no doubt that the Buddha's emphasis was on experience: the experience he had had himself and the experience he wanted others to have too. While he often appeals to reason, in the sense that he uses rational argument, the appeal to experience is even more important.[2]

Modern rationalist expositors like to draw attention to the *Kālāma Sutta* (AN III, 65 = AN I, 188-193), in which the Buddha advises the Kālāma clan not to accept any teaching merely on a teacher's authority, but to work things out for themselves.[3] However, he also proceeds to preach to them by

[1] See above, p. 16. It is only in poetry, in the last two books of the *Sutta-nipāta*, that the Buddha takes quietism to the point of claiming that he, or (more impersonally) the true sage, has no views (e.g. verses 787, 800, 882); and indeed it is to these poems that L.O. Gomez is referring in his article 'Proto-Mādhyamika in the Pali Canon' (Gomez, 1976). Steven Collins, who has devoted a whole excellent chapter (4) of his book *Selfless Persons* (Collins, 1982) to 'views' in the Canon, puts it well: 'these poems represent the summation, in Theravāda literature, of the style of teaching which is concerned less with the content of views and theories than with the psychological state of those who hold them' (p. 129).

[2] At the beginning of the *Mahā Sīhanāda Sutta* (MN I, 68) the Buddha sounds extremely annoyed when he is told what a man called Sunakkhatta is saying about him: that he teaches a doctrine for the extinction of suffering, and it does indeed have that effect, but that he has worked out that doctrine by his own powers of reasoning and has had no insight beyond the human norm. This text could be described as a rebuff to a purely rationalist interpretation of the Buddha. However, the tone of the entire text is such that I wonder whether one can read it as the Buddha's own words. The text is devoted to stressing the Buddha's extraordinariness, so that it reads as part of a debate on whether the Buddha was basically a normal human being.

[3] See also MN I, 265: 'Surely, monks, you should only say what you have found out, seen and understood for yourselves'.

asking them at each step whether they agree; he is appealing to their experience – we might also call it their common sense. Moreover, the content of the sermon is to show that morality has practical advantages. Again, the text is pragmatic and anti-theoretical.

Of other texts with this theme, let me particularly cite the *Tevijja Sutta* (DN *sutta* xiii), a text of which I shall have more to say later in the chapter. In this text the Buddha sharply criticises brahmins who say they know the path leading to union with Brahmā though they have never been there or seen Brahmā themselves. He compares them to the blind leading the blind (p. 239), and to someone who declares he is in love with the most beautiful woman in the country but cannot say, when asked, where she is or anything about her, for he has never seen her (pp. 241-2). The brahmins here being ridiculed are described as *tevijja*, 'having three knowledges'. The reference is to knowing by heart the three texts which alone brahmins considered to be true knowledge, and hence called Knowledge: the Ṛg, Sāma and Yajur Vedas. (To this day, the title accorded to a man who has the three texts by heart is found as a common brahmin surname: Trivedi, Tripathi, Tiwari etc..)

The *suttas* are artefacts, not perfect records of actual conversations. Our *Tevijja Sutta* does not include an interesting point which, its name suggests, may originally have been in it. That is that the Buddha himself claimed to have three knowledges; but his knowledges were not texts, but things he had experienced. The final stages of the path to Enlightenment, as set forth for example in the *Sāmañña-phala Sutta*, are articulated as a set of three knowledges (*vijjā*): knowledge of one's former lives; of the rebirths of others; and of the four noble truths and the destruction of the corruptions. There is no reason why this particular set of attainments – of which the last one is indeed composite – should be called 'three knowledges' if they were not intended to parallel and trump the 'three knowledges' of brahmins. That they are so intended is set out in AN *sutta* III 58 = AN I, 163-6, a sermon in which a brahmin called 'Three Ears'

(Tikaṇṇa) allegedly asks the Buddha on what basis a brahmin is said to be *tevijja*. One can hardly imagine a brahmin asking that question, and I believe that the brahmin's name establishes that this is a joke. But the sermon is a typical instance of the appropriation of brahmin terminology.

On the other hand, there certainly are plenty of 'right views' in the Canon, and enough material to fuel philosophical discussion, albeit intermittently, for more than two thousand years (and no doubt more to come). Many of the most famous and interesting sermons show the Buddha in dialogue, but after adapting what he has to say to the views of his opponents he often ends up by saying something positive in his own right. Moreover, one gets the feeling that in his wish to be pragmatic the Buddha is holding back. When he says (SN V, 437-8) that what he has explained compared to what he has not is like a handful of leaves compared to a whole forest, and he has explained only the four noble truths, I suspect a certain poignancy: that he would have enjoyed explaining more, had he not felt that it would distract his disciples from what mattered most. But one has to object that surely he did explain more, and that on the other hand it must be – has been – possible to achieve Enlightenment without understanding the chain of dependent origination.

I cannot finally resolve this problem of whether the Buddha was a philosopher *malgré lui*; and maybe it cannot be solved.[4] But I would like to revert to two Popperian concepts: unintended consequences and the logic of the situation.[5] Tradition has it that the Buddha, on attaining nirvana, wanted just to enjoy his condition and not to bother with preaching. (I suppose it felt a bit like coming back to class after sabbatical leave.) The texts also contain a quietist streak, especially in some of the poems in the

[4] I am not asking whether we should *call* the Buddha a philosopher; that is just a matter of definition, a pseudo-problem. My question concerns his intentions.

[5] The logic of the situation is the same as the rationality principle; see Gombrich, 1971:12-14. For these concepts see Popper, 1952:93-97 and Popper, 1974:120-135.

Sutta-nipāta (see note 1). But once his compassion had led him to share his experience with suffering creatures, he found himself involved in social intercourse for forty-five years. Even the Enlightened, I believe, have moods, and in some moods the Buddha was inclined to talk and to teach more than was absolutely necessary. It is the logic of the situation that that happens when people get together, and especially when a man finds himself surrounded by eager disciples, or challenged by intelligent disputants. Once a dialogue has started, answers must be found. Thus I suppose that what we now call Buddhist philosophy emerged, strictly speaking, as an unintended consequence of the Buddha's preaching; and that that emergence must have begun with the Buddha himself.[6]

* * *

I am not trying to write a textbook, so I want to say no more than is absolutely necessary about well known facts. The central teachings of the Buddha came as a response to the central teachings of the old Upaniṣads, notably the *Bṛhadāraṇyaka*. On some points, which he perhaps took for granted, he was in agreement with the Upaniṣadic doctrine; on other points he criticised it.

Let me put the relevant Upaniṣadic teachings as succinctly as I can:

1. Man is reborn according to the quality of his works (*karman*). 'Works' refers to following ritual prescriptions.[7] The typical *karman* is a sacrifice; this is normally positive. Violating a ritual norm is negative. Each such act has a given, finite result, positive

[6] On unintended consequences in the history of religions see Gombrich, 1988b:16-18.

[7] Traces of ethicisation of karma appear at *Bṛhadāraṇyaka Upaniṣad* 4, 4. But, despite Buddhist influence, brahminism has never thoroughly ethicised the concept or completely separated ethics from ritual.

or negative: a purifying act will be rewarded, a bad/polluting act punished. The most important forms of such reward and punishment are long-term: rebirth in higher or lower forms of life. Such higher and lower forms are on earth and in heaven(s) and hell(s), but all are temporary.

2. The only escape from this cycle of rebirth is by gnosis of a hidden truth, *brahman*, which is the esoteric meaning of the sacred texts (the Vedas). That truth is to be realised = understood during life, and this will lead to its being realised = made real at death. He who understands *brahman* will become *brahman*. In a less sophisticated form of this doctrine, *brahman* is personified, and the gnostic at death joins Brahman somewhere above the highest heaven.

3. The truth to be realised is about the nature of reality. The microcosm (man) mirrors the macrocosm (the universe). Both have an essence, a true nature, a 'self' (*ātman*), which is the same for both. So at the cosmic level *brahman* and *ātman* are to be understood as synonyms.

4. Being an essence, that *ātman* is unchanging: it is being as opposed to becoming. Being is also a plenum, since it can be predicated of everything that exists. Unhappiness is always due to a lack of something; being, a plenum, can lack nothing; therefore being has no unhappiness, but is bliss.

5. Ontology is merged (we might say confused) with epistemology, as can be seen from the double meaning of 'realised' given above. A truth (*satya*) is at the same time an existent (*sat*); indeed, it is existence (*sat* again), since existence is only one. Essentially we are existent, but we are also conscious of that truth. So existence is conscious (*cit*), or rather consciousness (*vijñāna*).

I think that this exposition shows that the doctrine of *karman* is fundamental to the entire structure. Similarly, I have frequently argued that the Buddha's doctrine of *karman* is fundamental to the structure of his thought. The Buddhist tradition selected the four noble truths as the most basic teaching (and so put that in the first sermon), but the Buddhist tradition *presupposes* that we are all being reborn according to the quality of our acts and that we wish to be released from this cycle of rebirth. Or, to put it another way, the first noble truth embodies the same assumption. The first noble truth is the single word *dukkha*, and it is explicated to mean that everything in our experience of life is ultimately unsatisfactory, so that it follows that for true satisfaction we must look outside that experience.

The Buddha taught that life as we experience it, phenomenal existence, has three hallmarks: that it is impermanent (*anicca*), unsatisfactory (*dukkha*) and not the 'self' (*anatta*). This is to accept the Upaniṣadic reasoning of paragraphs 3 and 4 above. The three hallmarks are corollaries of each other. What changes is by definition not the self, not an essence, and that it is unsatisfactory also comes very close to being true by definition. What gives the first noble truth its emotional force is its application to human life and the reminder that that always ends in death.

The Buddha thus accepted the Upaniṣadic dichotomy between the changing, unsatisfactory world of phenomena and its logically deduced opposite. However, after accepting the dichotomy he denied that the latter half of it existed – as a thing.

One could also argue that he accepted the macrocosm-microcosm equivalence – in a negative sense. The Upaniṣads reduced both to a single essence and then drew the equation 1 = 1. The Buddha, denying an essence in either sphere, drew a parallel equation: 0 = 0. The common sense view of the reality of things in the external world is not denied, though also not affirmed; it seems rather to be side-stepped as irrelevant theorising.[8] Since his teaching is intended to be pragmatic and concern itself with the problems of living beings, it is not surprising that there is no text in which he explicitly argues for a lack of essence to the universe; on this point he merely makes fun of the Upaniṣads – acting the Prāsaṅgika, we might say.

* * *

If I am right in thinking that the Buddha left no clear statement about the ontological status of the world – about what 'really' exists – this would explain how later Buddhists could disagree about this question. The early schools were what one might call (without pejorative intention) naive realists, and were severely criticised for this by Mahāyānist philosophers.

I suggest that the development of a Buddhist ontology, perhaps contrary to the Buddha's intentions, might be traced through considering the history of how the word *dhamma* is used. Two whole books on this problem exist already (Geiger & Geiger, 1920; Carter, 1978) and I have no wish to add a third, but I shall be rash enough here to outline a theory.

In brahminical thought, the word *Dharma*, in the singular, denotes a concept not unlike Nature in mediaeval European thought, a blend of what is and what should be the case. (In other words, the concept obliterates the fact/value distinction.) Brahminical philosophy came to posit categories of things classified by their essences (*sva-dharma*, 'own nature'). One's nature is at the same time one's duty. In principle there is a finite number of such essences (and duties) and in total they equal *Dharma* in the singular. In principle, again, all this is knowable – and indeed known by the liberated saint. This view is shared by brahminical illusionists (monists) and realists (pluralists); they disagree only on whether the essences are ultimately real.

[8] I return to this problem below, p. 94.

The original Buddhist Dharma/Dhamma is like the brahminical Dharma in having two facets. When the Buddha preached the Dharma, that was at the same time a true account (of experience) and a message what to do about it; it was at the same time descriptive and normative. The Pali Canon does not use the term *sva-dharma*, or what would be its Pali equivalent, and has no such concept, because the Buddha did not deal in essences. Nevertheless, *dhammā* occurs very often indeed in the plural. How so?

When the word refers to what the Buddha taught, there is no important difference between the singular and the plural, just as in English there is no important difference between the Buddha's Teaching and his Teachings. This has been illustrated in chapter 1 (p. 24) in the context of the raft simile.

The same word can lose its descriptive facet and simply mean a rule. This meaning need not concern us further.

On the other hand, the commonest use of the plural seems to lose the normative aspect of the word and be purely descriptive. In this sense *dhammā* refers to the contents of thought; just as sights are the objects of seeing or sounds of hearing, *dhammā* are the objects of thinking. In early Buddhism there are six senses; the mind (*manas*) is treated on a par with the other five. (Physical sense organs are accepted, but sense perception is not reified.) This sense of *dhammā* is so general that it is hard to translate: 'noeta' would be accurate but is too technical and obscure for most contexts; some favour 'phenomena', but that has misleading anti-realist implications; often the best translation is simply 'things'. But how did the word acquire this meaning?

Steven Collins (1982:115) has written: '*Dhammā* here are both elements of the normative system to be applied, and "objects" of experience in insight meditation.' I would pursue this line of thought even further. In the fundamental texts on meditation, the *Satipaṭṭhāna* and *Mahā Satipaṭṭhāna Suttas*, the meditator has to train himself to see reality as the Buddha has taught it to be. He is to do this in four stages. First he learns to observe physical processes in his own and other people's bodies; then he learns to be similarly aware of feelings; then of states of mind. Finally he learns to be aware of *dhammā* (plural). This has been rendered as 'his thoughts'. But the *dhammā* that the text spells out are in fact the teachings of the Buddha, such as the four noble truths. The meditator moves from thinking *about* those teachings to thinking *with* them: he learns (to use an anachronistic metaphor) to see the world through Buddhist spectacles. The Buddha's teachings come to be the same as (any) objects of thought, because anything else is (for Buddhists) unthinkable. Thus the *dhammā* are the elements of reality as understood by the Buddha.

My theory is that the term became generalised from this specific context of meditation. This does not yet mean that the *dhammā* have to be conceived ontologically, as things; indeed, many of them are propositions. The early texts, no doubt following the Buddha, do show a tendency to classify phenomena, especially according to the six senses, but there is no suggestion that within this classification (or others) the number of kinds of things is finite. This open-endedness contrasts with the closed universe of brahminical *sva-dharmas*. Moreover, to classify the world according to the senses by which it is perceived is not merely anthropocentric: it also emphasises *how* rather than *what* – how we know, and how we experience, rather than what there is.

A word about the subsequent history of *dhammā* (plural). In Sanskrit, the language of brahmin learning, *dharmāḥ* in the plural, acquired the meaning (among others) of 'noeta'. My hypothesis is that this usage came from Buddhism and that within brahmin thinking it originated in the school of *vaiśesika* philosophy, which in its theory of sense perception has similarities to Buddhism. For the *Vaiśeṣika* school, certain *dharmāḥ* are ultimately real entities. This is not unlike the realistic pluralism of early Buddhist systematised thought, the *abhidhamma*.

Ontology began to creep back into Buddhism, I suspect, when texts were compiled making lists of things the Buddha had referred to. These lists came to be thought of as an inventory of what the Buddha had taught to *exist*, as the building blocks of the universe. One could reduce only so far: all liquids were 'really' water (or, one could say, 'liquid' in general – the term 'water' might be figurative), but water could not be further reduced. There were many more abstract than concrete *dhammā*, and some were still the names of processes, like anger, but the list was a closed one. Thus the number of kinds of things in the world was taken to be established (though the various schools disagreed about the exact number), even though the number of instances of those things could not be. Thus, while the Buddhist *abhidhamma* remained opposed to Upaniṣadic monism, in this respect its world came to resemble the brahminical world with its *sva-dharmas*. This led to Nāgārjuna's reaction against essentialism, a reaction which I believe to have been in the spirit of the Buddha's intention.

* * *

Let me return to the Buddha – or as close to him as we can get. There is the same contrast between Buddhism and brahminism on the moral as on the ontological level. Sanskrit mythological texts reflect the idea that the world is a plenum in which good and evil, happiness and suffering are in balance, so that if the equilibrium is disturbed it must be restored. This is after all the basic idea behind ascetic practices (*tapas*): that if one inflicts deprivation on oneself now it will earn one good things later. Buddhism rejects these ideas. The only area in which it preserves this idea of a cosmic balance is in the law of *karma*, the law by which good deeds will be rewarded and bad deeds punished in the end.[9] Here, however, the equilibrium asserts itself within the moral continuum of the individual (which may last any number of lives) and the results are the responsibility of that individual, not imposed by an impersonal destiny.

[9] I have been criticised for using the terms 'reward' and 'punishment', both here and on p. 32 above, because the process is impersonal. The impersonal process can however legitimately be seen from our point of view.

In its open-endedness Buddhism is also in marked contrast to Jainism. Jains are fond of cosmological diagrams, which show a completely closed universe, bounded (by specified distances) both vertically and horizontally. The contents of this universe are also exhaustively classified. The Buddhist universe, by contrast, is unbounded in both spatial dimensions. Even though Theravādin scholasticism came to specify the number of heavens and hells, there is an irreduceable vagueness at the top and there is no top of the universe (*bhavagga*), as there is in Jainism. In the early Mahāyāna texts the universe seems to explode in all four dimensions, but this does no violence to the spirit of the earliest texts. To discuss time here would take me too far afield but I shall return to it in the next chapter.

* * *

I return to the microcosm. The Buddha does not often use ontological language at all. The most explicit passage in which he denies the *existence* of the *ātman* is in the *Alagaddūpama Sutta*. Perhaps the most famous of all Upaniṣadic dicta is *tat tvam asi* (*Chāndogya Upaniṣad* 6, 8, 7 etc.), 'Thou art that' – identifying the individual self/essence with the world self/essence. The transposition of this statement into the first person – 'I am this' – in Pali gives us *eso 'ham asmi*, and this is said in several texts to be false. To be precise, the full false statement is *etaṃ mama, eso 'ham asmi, eso me attā*: 'This is mine, I am this, this is my self/essence.' While this set of three clauses[10] is often mentioned as a wrong view, it is in the *Alagaddūpama Sutta* that it is most clearly amplified (at MN I, 135-6), and in terms which contain

[10] Dr Tuvia Gelblum has shown that virtually the same set of three clauses, adapted to meet the exigencies of the *āryā* metre, is found as *kārikā* 64 of the *Sāṃkhya Kārikā*. In that context they refer to realising that the *puruṣa* (spirit) neither is nor possesses any of the evolutes of *prakṛti* (nature). Gelblum, 1970:78-80.

other obvious verbal echoes of surviving Upaniṣadic passages.[11] Since both my teacher, Professor Norman, and I have published analyses of this passage in recent years (Norman, 1981; Gombrich, 1990), I shall not repeat them here. In sum, the passage denies that one's self is the same as the world and that one will become the world self at death. The Buddha tells the monks that people worry about something that is non-existent externally (*bahiddhā asati*) and non-existent internally (*ajjhattaṃ asati*); he is referring respectively to the soul/essence of the world and of the individual.

Though the above is probably the most important of all texts on this topic, I would here like to draw attention to two others which are perhaps less well known. Firstly: there is a passage in the *Aṅguttara Nikāya* (II, 212) which gives eighteen thoughts permeated by desire about the inner self and eighteen such thoughts about the external self. The text is unfortunately a bit corrupt (maybe because of the awkwardness of using some parts of the verb as 'to exist' in Pali), and the standard translation by Mrs Rhys Davids inept. Let me however offer a tentative translation:

'Monks, there are these eighteen considerations of craving with regard to what is internal to oneself[12], and eighteen with regard to what is external to oneself.

Internal: When there is the thought 'I am', there arise the thoughts: 'I am like this', 'I am like that', 'I am otherwise', 'I am non-existent'; 'I am existent'[13]; 'May I be'; 'May I be like this'; 'May I be like that'; 'May I be otherwise'; 'I might be'; 'I might be like this'; 'I might be like that'; 'I might be otherwise'; 'I shall be'; 'I shall be like this'; 'I shall be like that'; 'I shall be otherwise'.

[11] These echoes are not mentioned by the commentaries and seem not to have been noticed before modern times. They are mentioned by Hermann Oldenberg 1923:258.

[12] I interpret *ajjhattikassa upādāya* as a contraction for *ajjhattikaṃ assa upādāya*, and *bāhirassa* analogously as *bāhiraṃ assa*. *Upādāya* never seems to govern the genitive.

[13] As F. L. Woodward points out in his footnotes (Woodward, 1933:226), the commentary has got these two the wrong way round because it does not recognise the forms.

External: When there is the thought 'Through this I am', there arise the thoughts: 'Through this I am like this'; etc. etc.'

The text is the same except that each thought begins 'through this' (*iminā*). I feel particularly uncertain about how to translate *iminā*, but in the context it must refer to one's relation with the world soul/essence.

The Buddha concludes by saying that those caught in the web of these thirty-six considerations are tied up in knots and never escape from the round of rebirth. Though the passage is not entirely clear, it is perfectly clear that the basic wrong move is to think 'I am' (*asmi*) – perhaps better, 'I exist'. While the purpose of this is of course primarily soteriological, it seems to me to be a radical attack on the whole enterprise of constructing an ontology. The Buddha was attacking Vedānta and in effect denying Descartes: from the fact that there is a process of thinking he would refuse to draw the conclusion that 'I exist'. But remember that for the Buddha existence implies stasis: it is the opposite of becoming.

Both the above passages are referring to the Upaniṣads. Their doctrine of the essential identity between the individual and the world evolved through speculation in the Brāhmaṇa texts about the meaning of the sacrifice. The individual self with which these texts are concerned is that of the sacrificer, who is sacrificing in the hope of attaining heaven when he dies. In the oldest brahminical texts, that life in heaven was held to be eternal (as, for instance, in Christianity). The Buddha seems to have known these more archaic texts too.

In the *Taittirīya Saṃhitā*, one of the recensions of the Black Yajur Veda, are instructions for building a fire altar. The sacrificer is told to lay in the middle a brick which is smeared with dung, 'for truly, dung is the middle of the self. It is with his self that he lays the fire. He who knows this comes to be in the other world with his self' (V, 3, 5, 2). The word I have translated 'self' is *ātman*; the reference is clearly to a physical body. In the middle of the body are faeces; he who understands this is re-embodied in heaven.

In one text in the Pali Canon (SN III, 144), the Buddha holds up before some monks a pellet of cow dung. (The commentary (SA II, 324) seems a bit shocked that he should be handling dung and suggests that he produced it there and then by supernormal power.) He has just said – as so often – that nothing in the five groups of components of a person (*khandha*) is permanent, stable, exempt from change. Showing the dung pellet, he says that one does not acquire a self even of this size which is permanent, etc.; if one did, one would not live this holy life to destroy suffering. He goes on to talk of a former life in which he was an emperor; but now that glory has all passed away.

I suspect that the Buddha is here alluding to the Vedic doctrine. This is made the more likely, it seems to me, by the somewhat awkward phraseology of the Pali. The self in Pali is usually *attā*, but here the word used is *attabhāva*, which commonly means the body, or rather the person, in a particular life. What I have translated as 'one does not acquire a self' is in Pali *attabhāva-paṭilābho n' atthi*; the *P.E.D.* translates *attabhāva-paṭilābho* 'assumption of an existence, becoming reborn as an individual'. It is not quite logical to say that the assumption of a particular physical existence is not permanent and liable to change; obviously that predicate applies to the physical existence, not to the assumption. But if the words are alluding to a doctrine about creating a physical existence in the next world, an existence which is in some sense the same as one's present self, the use of this vocabulary becomes transparent.

Incidentally, this affords a good illustration of how the Pali Canon was formed. In the very next *sutta* the Buddha takes a little dirt in his fingernail and says that even this much of the five *khandha* – he goes through them in turn – is not permanent, stable, etc.; if it were, there would be no holy life. Most of the text is identical to the previous *sutta*. That contains an oddity, which this text has ironed out. The resultant *sutta*, proclaiming the total impermanence of each of the five *khandha*, is banal, exactly repeating the message found in many other texts. We are lucky that the latter sermon has not replaced the former one, but merely been added to it. This process of levelling out, of banalisation, illustrates the principle (alluded to in my first chapter) of *lectio difficilior potior*, that the more difficult reading is the one likely to be original.

* * *

I believe in criticism and debate, so before I go further I should make some acknowledgment of the widely-held view that in fact the Buddha's soteriology was as close to the Vedānta of the early Upaniṣads as makes no difference. One of the arguments used is that the Pali texts contain some characteristic Vedāntin terminology. The best example is that an Enlightened person is said to live *brahma-bhūtena attanā*, 'with his self/essence become brahman' (e.g. AN II, 211). The Buddha himself is said to be *brahma-bhūto*, 'become brahman' (e.g. MN I, 111). My answer is at the most general level, as explained in my first chapter: that the Buddha regularly used the language of his opponents, but turned it into metaphor. Examples simply pullulate, because in soteriology metaphors are inevitable. What the Buddha taught we may consider a perfect example of a soteriology; only the most perverse pedant would object that it was not a soteriology at all, because the Greek word *sōtēr* means 'saviour' and the Buddha was not a saviour, just a teacher who explained how one could save oneself. Similarly, at MN I, 111, a few words after the Buddha is called *brahma-bhūto*, he is also called *amatassa dātā*, 'giver of the immortal' – another metaphor, very close to 'saviour'.

One should always try to respond to one's opponent's strongest argument. In my view the strongest argument of those who want to make the Buddha a Vedāntin or quasi-Vedāntin lies in the brief passage in the *Udāna* (VIII, 3 = pp. 80-81) which runs: 'There is, monks, an unborn, unbecome, unmade, uncompounded; if there were not, there would be known no escape here from the born, become, made, compounded.'

The *Udāna* is an anthology, much of it culled from other extant texts. It is hard not to be sceptical about its antiquity. Its first pages are the same as those of the *Mahāvagga* of the *Vinaya Khandhaka*, and the *Udāna* is obviously the borrower from that extended (and largely allegorical) narrative (see chapters 1 and 3). I accept Frauwallner's finding that the *Khandhaka* must have been composed soon after the Second Communal Recitation (Frauwallner, 1956:54; Gombrich, 1988a); so the *Udāna* must be even later.

The chief problem with interpreting the passage is that it comes to us in complete isolation, with no context. If it was a direct response to a brahmin who, say, accused the Buddha of denying all possibility of salvation, the language would be quite understandable. After all, we have already seen that the Buddha largely accepted the Upaniṣadic analysis of this phenomenal world, and to state its opposite is a mere logical deduction. It is only the first word, *atthi*, 'there exists', which seems a bit troublesome, and one notices that it is not repeated in asserting the escape: that 'is known' (*paññāyati*), again emphasising subjective experience. In the end I think one simply has to weigh the evidence and conclude that though this statement, plucked from an unknown context, may sound like Vedānta, there is insufficient reason to take it as ontology rather than logic: the bare argument that if there is a process it must also be possible to conceive of a cessation of that process.

A fundamental difference between the Buddha's view and the Upaniṣadic view is that the Buddha never confused epistemology with ontology. (At least, he did not do so at the philosophical level; the meaning of this qualification will become clear in the next chapter.) The Buddha did not reify consciousness. *Viññāṇa* is one of the five *khandha*, and is a process, not a thing: consciousness is always consciousness *of*. Pure consciousness is just an abstraction.

However, just as there is one statement in the Canon which has been taken to reify nirvana, there is one verse which has often been taken to reify consciousness. Moreover, it has been taken to privilege consciousness, in the Upaniṣadic manner, as the supreme reality; in other words, to express an idealistic ontology. The later idealistic school of Buddhist philosophy, the *Vijñāna-vāda*, seized on this text as its authority. But again, there is so much evidence in the Canon pointing in the opposite direction that we should see whether this verse must necessarily express idealism or whether some other interpretation is plausible.

The verse occurs in the *Kevaddha Sutta* (*sutta* xi) of the *Dīgha Nikāya*. It comes as the conclusion and climax to a narrative, and it is the answer to a riddle for which a monk has been seeking a solution. The beginning of the *sutta* concerns the exercise of super-normal powers (*iddhi*), which the Buddha condemns as vulgar conjuring tricks, so the topic of making things disappear fits the context. The riddle (which is also in verse) runs:

> Where do earth, water, fire and wind
> find no footing?
> Where are long and short, subtle and
> gross, pure and impure,
> Where are name and form entirely destroyed?

(The expression 'name and form', Dr. Hamilton has shown (1993:206-231), refers to all individual existence: form is physical (not necessarily visible) identity, name conceptual identity.)

The answer, in five lines of verse, runs:

> Consciousness has no attribute, is infinite,
> luminous to every side.
> Here do earth, water, fire and wind find
> no footing.
> Here are long and short, subtle and gross,
> pure and impure,
> Here are name and form entirely destroyed.
> By the cessation of consciousness this here is
> destroyed'. (p. 223)

It is a bit risky to take a riddle or its solution as a philosophical tenet or argument. Certainly, however, the opening statement of the answer seems *prima facie* to reify consciousness and the language sounds as if it could come from an Upaniṣad. But this is not the only possible interpretation. Consciousness is, for the Buddha, a process which illuminates objects. So when there is nothing to illuminate, there is no illumination: 'consciousness has no attribute' (*anidassanaṃ*).

When is there nothing to illuminate? There are several passages in the Canon which in part parallel this one, and together they answer this question. Both the second and fourth lines occur, separately or together, in several other short poems.[14] Another passage (Ud VIII, 1 = p. 80) says that there exists a state (*āyatana*) in which there is no... – and there follows a long list, beginning with the elements, including 'this world and the next' and ending with 'mental objects' (*ārammaṇa*); and this alone is the end of suffering. Like the statement discussed just above, which it precedes, this is a short prose passage quoted in the *Udāna* without any context. Here however the language – 'a state' which is 'the end of suffering' – sounds less distinctively Upaniṣadic. In all these passages the reference is to nirvana, the condition in which consciousness of duality and hence of specific entities has been transcended. This does not mean that consciousness is a thing which exists independently of its operations, let alone that other entities depend on it for their existence.

* * *

The Buddha's interest in how not what, his emphasis on processes rather than objects, could be said to be summarised in his teaching of the *paṭicca-samuppāda*, conditioned origination.

[14] Line 2: Ud I, 10 = p. 9. Line 4: SN *sutta* I, 3, 3 = SN I, 13; SN *sutta* I, 5, 10 = SN I, 35. Both: SN *sutta* I, 3, 7 = SN I, 15. I ignore variations in the first word of the line.

There is an enormous literature on this doctrine and I have no ambition to make any substantial addition to it. I would however like to note in passing that I consider Frauwallner to have made a very useful contribution when he pointed out (Frauwallner, 1973:167) that the full twelve-link formulation combines the theory that our troubles are all due to ignorance (the intellectualist analysis) with the theory that they are due to desire (the emotionalist analysis), a matter relevant to chapter 4 below.

There is something I find odd about the *paṭicca-samuppāda*. On the one hand many texts make it the central point of the Buddha's teaching. At MN I, 190-1 Sāriputta says that the Buddha said that to see (i.e. understand) the *paṭicca-samuppāda* and to see his teaching are the same; and – accordingly? – the content of the Buddha's Enlightenment is given in some texts not as the four noble truths and the destruction of the corruptions but as conditioned origination.[15] On the other hand there is considerable disagreement about how to interpret the doctrine, and the texts themselves seem to acknowledge this, for the classic exposition of it, in the *Mahā-nidāna Sutta* (DN *sutta* xv) is preceded by the Buddha's telling Ānanda that it is far from clear. Ānanda says (DN II, 55), 'It is marvellous and wonderful how profound this conditioned origination is and how profound it appears. And yet to me it seems quite clear.' The Buddha replies, 'Don't say that, Ānanda. This conditioned origination is profound and appears profound. It is through not understanding this teaching that people are enmeshed and cannot escape from the round of rebirth.' Similarly, after initially discovering it, the Buddha is represented as thinking that it is so hard to understand that it is not worth his while to try to teach it (Vin I, 4 = MN I, 167). Nevertheless, he does teach it to Ānanda – who, by tradition, was not Enlightened during the Buddha's lifetime, and so presumably did not understand it.

[15] I assume this version of the Enlightenment to be the later one. It opens the *Mahāvagga* of the *Vinaya Khandhaka*, and the *Udāna*.

Certainly, if one thing is clear about the doctrine of conditioned origination it is that even in the Pali Canon it has several interpretations. What they have in common is that the doctrine explains processes, and how they occur in a non-random manner.

The clearest statement that consciousness is simply a process expresses this fact by saying that it is dependently originated (*paṭicca-samuppanna*). In the *Mahā-taṇhā-saṅkhaya Sutta* (MN *sutta* 38) a monk called Sāti has understood the Buddha to have taught that in the process of rebirth the same consciousness is reborn without change. Sāti's opinion is reported in exactly the same terms as Ariṭṭha's at the beginning of the *Alagaddūpama Sutta*. Ariṭṭha, as I recounted in chapter 1, said his interpretation of the Buddha's teaching was that sexual intercourse was no bar to the holy life, i.e., to being a monk. Sāti's view that consciousness transmigrates is likewise characterised as a wicked view (*pāpakaṃ diṭṭhi-gataṃ*), and the narrative follows the same course: after trying to disabuse him, monks report him to the Buddha, who summons him and castigates him roundly for a misunderstanding 'which both damages himself and generates much demerit' (p. 259).

The Buddha says of both (pp. 132, 258) that they have no inkling (literally: 'they are not warmed up', *usmī-kato*) of his doctrine and discipline. The Buddha even alludes to his teaching being like a raft, without explication (p. 261), which indicates that this text is the borrower. It is interesting that believing in an unchanging consciousness is put on a par with denying the practical foundation of monasticism. At the end of the *sutta* (p. 271), the Buddha tells the monks to regard Sāti as entangled in the mesh of craving; so his fault is not just intellectual but moral. This fits what we saw above in the text about thirty-six considerations: to hold ontological views about continued existence, in the Upaniṣadic manner, is regularly attributed to craving (*taṇhā*).

The Buddha says (p. 259) that he has explained in many ways that consciousness is dependently originated. It is categorised according to the cause that produced it (*yaṃ yad eva paccayaṃ paṭicca uppajjati viññāṇaṃ tena ten' eva saṅkhaṃ gacchati*). When it arises in dependence on the eye because of forms ('in dependence on' and 'because of' are both *paṭicca* in Pali, but to use either translation throughout seems to me to do violence to English usage) it is classed as 'eye consciousness', and so on through the six senses, ending with 'mind consciousness'. This is just like fire, which is classed according to its (material) cause as a wood fire, a grass fire, or whatever. I do not think the Buddha could have put it more clearly: no fuel, no fire; so if there is nothing to be conscious of there is no consciousness.[16]

A little later in the same text the Buddha says that there are four foods which keep living beings in the cycle of rebirth: food in the literal sense, contact, intention and consciousness. All four arise from craving, this in turn from feeling – and he traces dependent origination in the standard way back to ignorance. So here the dependence refers to a different process, or at least to a different part of the all-important process of our entanglement in the world, the process we have to reverse.

* * *

In seeing the teaching of dependent origination as the Buddha's answer to Upaniṣadic ontology I have kept within the framework of Buddhist dogmatics. By that token, what I have said is almost sure to be correct and uncontroversial, but is also not very new or interesting. I would like now to offer a different analysis, which does not repeat the formulations of the texts, but is I hope nevertheless valid and makes sense in a historical framework. This analysis is the claim that just as Being lies at the heart of the Upaniṣadic world view, Action lies at the heart of the Buddha's.

[16] At least in the normal sense! Consciousness of a condition transcending duality, i.e. subjects and objects, is not only beyond normal experience, but cannot be conceptualised. That is why such experiences can only be referred to by negation.

'Action', of course, is *kamma*; and primarily it refers to morally relevant action.

There is of course nothing original about seeing *kaṃma* as central to Buddhist ideology. The great Étienne Lamotte wrote: 'The doctrine of the act, karman, is the keystone of the entire Buddhist edifice; the act is the ultimate explanation of existences and of the world; the Buddhist philosophers built up their philosophies as a function of *karma*.' (Lamotte, 1935-6:151).

It may be wise to reassert Lamotte's position, because some anthropologists have tried to detach Buddhist karma doctrine from Buddhist soteriology and to see it as somehow secondary, linked perhaps with Weber's 'insufficiency ethic', a religious complex provided for those unable to strive for that religion's highest goals. For the pragmatic purpose of describing a particular Buddhist society this can be a valid tactic. In his description of Burmese Buddhism Melford Spiro coined the terms 'nibbanic Buddhism' and 'kammatic Buddhism' in order to organise his account (Spiro, 1970:12), and I see nothing wrong in that. However, I begin to disagree when the links between those two complexes are so attenuated that one becomes at least conceivable without the other; and this has happened in the work of Geoffrey Samuel, whose 'Bodhi Orientation' and 'Karma Orientation' are explicitly modelled on Spiro's distinction (Samuel, 1993:5-6). I am not taking issue with Samuel's very interesting account of Tibetan Buddhism. But he seems to think that the two complexes/orientations have separate historical roots. He writes of the beginnings of Buddhism: 'Karma was a commonplace of the various Indian philosophical schools of this period, and by no means a specifically Buddhist development....' 'There is an apparent contradiction between the doctrine of karma and the central insight of the Buddhist Enlightenment .... The latter involves a going beyond the desires, hatreds, and motivations of the everyday world. How can it be reconciled with a teaching in which certain actions are proper and to be cultivated, and others are not? The Buddhist answer to this paradox has remained essentially the same since the days of the early Sutras' (p. 378).

I think that there are here two linked misconceptions, one historical and one doctrinal. It is a historical misconception that the Buddha took over a pre-existing doctrine of karma, and a doctrinal misconception that there is an 'apparent contradiction' or 'paradox'.

History first. Samuel is of course right that so far as we can judge there were several doctrines of karma in existence at the time of the Buddha, not just the brahminical one. We know very little about any of the others except the Jain, and even for that much of our evidence is rather late. We can see that the Buddha was not even alone in opposing the brahmin concept of karma as ritual act with an ethical view: the Jains too held that karma had an intrinsic ethical value. For the Jains, however, karma was not simply good or bad; to a greater or lesser extent it was all bad. They conceptualised karma as a kind of dust or dirt which clung to the soul, which too was material, whenever one acted. The dust weighed down the soul and kept it in this world, eventually to be reborn in another body. Bad deeds were worse than good deeds, producing worse karmic dirt, but to attain liberation one had to expunge all karma from the soul so that it could float, weightless, to the top of the universe.

The theory that karma is somehow material resurfaced in Buddhism later, as we shall see. Though it seems curious, it has a certain logic to it. In all its forms, the theory of karma holds that an action produces a fitting result at some later time. Theism could hold that the fitting results are distributed by an agent, a god, whose memory would provide the necessary continuity. However, the early theories of karma all held that the results accrued without any further intervention. The analogy posited for this action at a distance was that of a seed and its fruit. To perform the act was to plant a seed, and though it was no longer visible (being, as it were, underground) it would germinate in due course.

Buddhist philosophers such as Vasubandhu made explicit and detailed use of this analogy between karma and seed, though for Vasubandhu it remained just an analogy (*Abhidharmakoṣa* IX). He remained true to the Buddha's doctrine that karma was an abstract process. The Buddha defined karma as intention; whether the intention manifested itself in physical, vocal or mental form, it was the intention alone which had a moral character: good, bad or neutral.

I have written at length elsewhere (Gombrich, 1988b:66-69) about how the Buddha's re-definition of 'action' as 'intention', an audacious use of language, turned the brahmin ideology upside down and ethicised the universe. I do not see how one could exaggerate the importance of the Buddha's ethicisation of the world, which I regard as a turning point in the history of civilisation. The Jains had taken a step in this direction, criticising brahmin concepts and especially animal sacrifice; but they were quietists, for whom, at least initially, even good deeds were preferably to be avoided.[17] For them, good actions truly constituted a Weberian insufficiency ethic. For Buddhists, they did not: their ideology was all of a piece.

'It is intention that I call karma' is the Buddha's answer to brahmin ritualism. The focus of interest shifted from physical action, involving people and objects in the real world, to psychological process. In brahminism, the opposite of an evil action (*pāpa*) was one which removed evil and pollution, which purified (*puṇya*);[18] typically such action involved washing. In Buddhism 'purification' became a dominant metaphor for spiritual progress. Buddhaghosa's great summary of Theravādin doctrine is called the *Visuddhi-magga*, 'The Path of Purification'.

[17] This is true of Jainism in the period of the Buddha and the Pali Canon, when doctrine made few if any concessions to lay needs. See Johnson, 1990:1-47.

[18] I am grateful to Dr Chlodwig Werba for pointing out that historically this adjective probably does not derive from the root *pū* 'purify'; but the Buddhists thought that it did.

Since *karman/kamma* is a basic item of vocabulary which literally means 'act', 'action', 'deed', and the Buddha's appropriation of the term thus flouts ordinary usage, it is not at all surprising that the texts about karma also show some linguistic confusion. Dogmatically, a monk's kind thought is good, purifying karma; but it does not come naturally to call it 'action'. This is the source of Samuel's doctrinal misconception. For clarity, one might differentiate between 'typical' karma, which is overt and has some effect on the external world, and 'dogmatic' karma, any morally charged physical, vocal or mental action.[19] The latter subsumes the former. *Kamma*, and related words like *puñña*, are used sometimes in the one and sometimes in the other sense: for example, *puñña kamma* is more used of 'typical' karma, *visuddhi* of 'dogmatic' karma, even though they both mean 'purifying'.

Good and bad *kamma* in contexts where the 'dogmatic' sense is uppermost tend to be called 'skilful' (*kusala*) and 'unskilful' (*akusala*) in that they show mastery, or lack of it, of the spiritual technology. Moreover, at the higher stages of progress, when one is normally a monk or nun, 'typical' karma tends to be phased out, since one is not moving in society but mainly living the life of the mind in meditation. The Enlightened person has not expunged karma, like a Jain saint, but no longer has any bad intentions and has rendered karma irrelevant, in that he or she is now beyond the stage where he/she could benefit from the maturation of good acts.

We can see the dilemma about how to talk about karma in a text in the *Aṅguttara Nikāya* (*sutta* III, 108 = I, 263). The previous *sutta* was about the three bad motivations for karma: greed, hatred and delusion. This *sutta* says:

[19] Though these terms for and explanations of the two types are my own, the distinction itself corresponds to one made by Buddhaghosa between 'finite' and 'boundless' karma. See below p. 85.

There are three causes for the arising of *kamma*: non-greed, non-hatred and non-delusion. The *kamma* done with one of these, caused by it, arising out of it, is skilful, not blameworthy, and brings happiness (*sukha-vipākaṃ*); it conduces to the destruction of *kamma*, not to the arising of *kamma*.

The karma at the beginning, that caused by non-greed etc., is 'dogmatic' karma. But it does not bring about its own destruction, as a literal reading of the text might suggest; it merely causes one to pass beyond the sphere of 'typical' karma, till – ideally – one reaches the level at which karma is irrelevant.

There is nothing strange or implausible about this dual conception of karma. Ordinary words are not always adequate to extraordinary circumstances; nor does philosophical analysis always find everyday language an adequate tool. There is a parallel to the problem with the term karma in the conceptualisation of motivation for acting. An ordinary unenlightened person acts from a certain desire (which may be positive or negative), and this has karmic consequences. Enlightened people, such as the Buddha, also act, and their actions are motivated, but not in a way that has karmic consequences, so that it does not seem quite right to say that they act out of any 'desire'. Contemporary philosophy has solved a closely analogous problem by introducing the term 'pro-attitude'. To quote a philosophy textbook:

To give someone's reason for acting .. we must typically mention a desire which he has and a corresponding belief to the effect that the action done is a means to securing the desired end .... However, isn't this formulation open to a rather obvious objection? For surely people sometimes intentionally do things which it would be odd to describe them as *desiring* to do.... So what we really need here is not the everyday notion of desire so much as the generalised semi-technical notion of a 'pro-attitude' .... (Smith & Jones, 1986:131)

The authors then quote Donald Davidson, who introduced this term for a notion of desire which is more generalised than the normal usage. Taking a leaf from Davidson's book, I would thus say that the 'dogmatic' notion of karma is a more generalised notion of karma in the same way as 'pro-attitude' supplies a more generalised notion of desire.

* * *

While Spiro and Samuel would obviously be right to say that my 'typical' karma is mainly connected to lay life and my 'dogmatic' karma to monastic life, this rough and ready social truth does not grasp the real distinction. On the one hand, Mumford's book *Himalayan Dialogue* (Mumford, 1989) shows the life of even lay Tibetan Buddhists permeated by an awareness of the crucial importance of ethical intention. On the other, Buddhist scholastics were worried about such matters as the karmic effect of the vocal act of taking monastic vows.

Let me briefly report on the latter,[20] because they provide an interesting example of how literalism led to doctrinal development; they also provide further evidence of how my distinction between 'typical' and 'dogmatic' karma, albeit a mere expository device, reflects a problem which constantly recurred in the history of Buddhism. The Sarvāstivāda was probably the most important of all pre-Mahāyāna Buddhist intellectual traditions; it seems to have predominated in many parts of India at least until the time of Vasubandhu (fifth century A.D.). It was divided into two: the Vaibhāṣikas followed the *abhidharma* of that school, being named after the *Mahā Vibhāṣā*, a commentary on part of their *Abhidharma Piṭaka*; the Sautrāntikas, on the other hand, regarded only the canonical *sūtras* as authoritative. The Sautrāntikas rejected the following Vaibhāṣika theory.

The full statement in which the Buddha defines *kamma* (AN III, 415) has two parts and runs as follows: 'Monks, it is intention that I call karma. By intending one performs karma

[20] My understanding of the Sarvāstivāda owes much to the Oxford lectures of Professor Alexis Sanderson.

through body, word or thought.' The two parts of the statement are virtually synonymous, for the second merely provides a slight amplification. This is the Sautrāntika view and I am sure it is true to the original meaning of the text. But the Vaibhāṣikas read more into the amplification. They separated the intention from the act, with the intention coming first. So karma became divided into two parts: intention and what happens next. Bodily and verbal action manifested one's intention to others and therefore were called *vijñapti*, 'information'.

The first part of the Vaibhāṣika karma corresponds to my 'dogmatic' karma; they regarded it as karma proper, because of the force of the first half of the Buddha's statement. The 'information' of the bodily or verbal action corresponds to my 'typical' karma.

Good or bad karma entails results for the doer. Buddhist philosophers wished to trace the mechanism of this entailment. The name Sarvāstivādin means 'maintaining that everything exists', i.e., exists in the present; it refers to the doctrine of this school that in some sense a past act was still present at the time when it yielded its result. On this both branches of the school agreed, but they differed on the further detail.

The Vaibhāṣikas had invented the 'information' physical or verbal act, but that was obviously short-lived. For example, a monk might enunciate his vows, an act providing information to those within earshot; but by what mechanism did the effect of that speech endure? They replied that it stayed with the agent as 'non-information' (*avijñapti*). As the agent was not constantly aware of all the non-information he was carrying, it could not be mental. However, the Sarvāstivādins had forgotten the Buddha's wisdom in bypassing ontology, and had classified everything (except space and nirvana) as either mental or physical. So 'non-information' karma had to be physical, though it consisted of a kind of matter perceptible only to consciousness, not to the other senses. Thus the Vaibhāṣikas came to resemble the Jains, in that they held that physical or vocal action generated karma in physical form.

In the Canon (SN I, 33) there is a six-line verse, which I translate as follows: 'Whose merit always increases day and night? What righteous, moral people go to heaven? People who plant parks and woods, who build bridges, who donate wells and cisterns and dwellings, their merit always increases day and night; those righteous, moral people go to heaven.' This question and answer have no context and are a simple exhortation to lay generosity; one would not tend to give the wording a second thought. But literalists took the words to mean that one's merit grows after one has made the donation. They asked themselves how this could be, and answered that every time someone benefits from a donation, more merit must accrue to the donor. Since the donor may be unaware of this access of merit, he has to have a non-mental property which is affected. This too is his 'non-information'.

For the Buddha's doctrine of intention, the use made of a donation is not relevant (as the Sautrāntikas realised). The Vaibhāṣika interpretation makes merit depend in part on factors over which the doer may have no control, and of which he may even be ignorant. Thus merit, good karma, is reified and turned into a spiritual analogue of money or some other hoardable commodity. It is when karma comes to be understood in this sense that there is a disjunction between its conceptualisation and Buddhist soteriology.

* * *

The transfer of karma – in particular of good karma, merit – is a vast topic; much has been written about it and there is no room here for a long digression. However, I cannot resist the opportunity to make three points. First: Buddhologists have tended to ignore the importance of such transfers in brahminical texts, where they are documented from a very early period. As Professor Hara has pointed out (Hara, 1994), the *Mahābhārata*, for example, envisages transfer not only of good and bad karma but of such things as long life and dishonour. So the idea that many properties we are accustomed to thinking of as non-transferable can in fact be transferred was probably part of a widespread popular belief, and in partly accepting it Buddhism was moving towards the general norm.

However, too easy acceptance of such transferability would have shaken the foundations of Buddhism as a doctrine of moral responsibility. So far from reifying merit, Buddhist orthodoxy even resisted the reification of the individual, the moral agent. How could a process transfer an aspect of itself to another process? The Sarvāstivāda, showing a tendency to multiply entities, argued that the process which we conventionally talk of as a person was connected to its properties (including karma) by something called *prāpti* 'possession' (in a verbal sense). The Theravāda came to accept the transfer of merit, but apparently tried to evade the problematic notion of transferring a process, karma, by taking over this piece of Sarvāstivādin terminology. This is my second point; I am not aware that it has been noticed before. In Pali, therefore, what is said to be given is not merit but 'possession' (of merit) – *patti-dāna*. Though all Theravādins use the term *patti* (= Sanskrit *prāpti*), I suspect that hardly any of them know just what it means (as distinct from what it refers to), since it was borrowed from another school.

In early Buddhism, the Buddha was a saviour only in the sense that he taught the way to salvation. In the Mahāyāna, both Buddhas and bodhisattvas saved more directly, by transferring merit. My third point is that this transfer of a reified karma seems to me to be what is crucial in turning Buddhism into a religion in which one could be saved by others. It is thus the transfer of merit which takes the place in Buddhism which divine grace occupies in Christianity.

* * *

When the reification of karma into a transferable commodity has been carried so far that it can be distributed to the wicked, the original doctrine of karma has been stood on its head. The logic of the ethic of intention has been subverted. But this does not necessarily mean that Buddhism has become unrecognisably changed in every respect. From the outset, the Buddha was said to be supremely compassionate. Moreover, there was said to be only one Enlightenment; so anyone who achieved Enlightenment should be in the same moral condition as the Buddha. Nevertheless, the Mahāyāna attacked earlier Buddhism for lack of warmth. It is true that the Buddha does not seem to have envisaged the possibility of handing out free merit, and hence salvation, to those who did not help themselves. So can the Mahāyāna criticism be just? The answer to that depends, I think, on how we interpret some of the earliest texts. We must go back to the *Tevijja Sutta*.

The Upaniṣadic soteriology centred on the static self, the Buddha's on dynamic moral agency. To realise the self as the only reality is to realise what has always been the case: change and movement were an illusion. In the Buddha's world, by contrast, one has to make things happen.

The less sophisticated brahmin, on the other hand, aimed to attain brahman at death in some less mystical way. In chapter 1 I have mentioned the god Brahmā, who personified the essence of brahminhood and dwelt in the highest heaven. (What sophisticated doctrine declares to transcend the world, the less sophisticated regularly interpret as being at the top of the world; the same occasionally happened to nirvana.) In the *Bṛhadāraṇyaka Upaniṣad* (6, 2, 15) those who have achieved gnosis go beyond the sun to the lightning when they die; thence they are conducted to the worlds of brahman (*brahma-lokān*) and stay there; they are never reborn. The compound noun in fact leaves open the possibility that the worlds they stay in are of

Brahmā, or even of Brahmās in the plural. It is to this interpretation that the Buddhist texts seem to be responding.[21]

In the *Tevijja Sutta* the Buddha is arguing with brahmins whose goal, the text alleges, is 'companionship with Brahmā' (*brahma-sahavyatā*) (first mentioned DN I, 235). The Buddha says (p. 240) that though they can see the sun and moon, they do not even know the way to joining them – let alone the way to Brahmā. I suspect that his remark about the sun and moon is a jocular allusion to the Upaniṣadic two paths at death;[22] jocular, because if the Buddha knew the doctrine he can hardly have failed to know that to take those paths one had to have one's corpse burnt first. When talking of joining Brahmā, he does mention that it happens after death (first at p. 245, para.25). He also seems to allude to the idea of becoming identical with brahman, because one argument he uses against the brahmins (pp. 247-8) is that they are utterly unlike Brahmā. Typically, the unlikeness he talks of is moral:[23] Brahmā, by the brahmins' account, is morally pure, but they are not, so how can they claim to match him?

The Buddha then tells his brahmin interlocutor that he knows the brahma-world and the way to it as well as if he had lived there all his life. The young brahmin replies that he has indeed heard that the Buddha teaches the way to companionship with Brahmās – note the plural; he asks to hear it. The Buddha proceeds to describe the way. He gives a standard account of how someone comes across the Buddha and his preaching, renounces the household life, and keeps all the rules of conduct and morality.

[21] In the *Chāndogya Upaniṣad* (5, 10, 2) the route is a bit different and they unambiguously reach *brahman*, neuter. Many allusions to the BĀU have now been traced, whereas the only one I know of to the ChU is to *tat tvam asi* (see p. 38), which must have been famous. I assume that here too the Buddha's allusions are to the BĀU.

[22] Two paths first mentioned: BĀU 6, 2, 2. The second, which finally leads to rebirth, is via the moon: 6, 2, 16. Those who do not know these two paths become (are?) worms and insects (*ibid.*).

[23] I think that the commentary has misinterpreted the first quality, *pariggaha*: it does not refer to material possessions (wives included) but to possessiveness, the propensity to have those possessions.

Then he describes how this person – now referred to as a monk – pervades every direction with thoughts of kindness, compassion, sympathetic joy and equanimity; in the usual style, the same description is repeated for each of the four kinds of thoughts. The four (in Pali *mettā*, *karuṇā*, *muditā* and *upekkhā)*, come to be referred to in other texts as *brahma-vihāra*, but that term is not used here.

Three words based on the word for 'all' (*sabba*-) are used to stress the entirety of the pervasion, and the thought is said to be 'extensive, magnified, boundless, without hatred or ill will' (*vipulena mahaggatena appamāṇena averena avyāpajjhena*). These five adjectives amount to saying that it is pure unalloyed kindness and infinite in extent. It is compared to the noise made by a powerful conch-blower. (The point of this is that sound, unlike the objects of the other senses, is considered to be infinite and to pervade all space.)

Then kindness (followed by the other three in turn) is described as 'release of the mind' (*ceto-vimutti*); when it has been thus developed, no bounded (i.e., finite) karma remains there. The text (p. 251 para.77) repeats the last point for emphasis. This is the way to companionship with Brahmās (plural). A monk who lives like this (*evaṃ-vihārī*) matches Brahmā (singular) in his moral qualities, so that he joins him at death.

In the introduction to his translation of the *sutta* Rhys Davids (1899:298-9) correctly noted that this text is 'the Buddhist answer to the Upanishad theory' and an *argumentum ad hominem*; but oddly enough nobody seems to have read the text closely enough to catch all the parallels and hence the full significance of what is being said. The fact that Rhys Davids (untypically) completely mistranslated the repeated clause in para.77 may not have helped.

I have above translated the word *cetas/ceto* as both 'thought' and 'mind'. 'Mind' will normally do very well, provided one does not forget that the Buddha did not think of it as an object but as the process of thinking. In chapter 4 I discuss *ceto-vimutti* at length, and show that in the early texts it is simply a term for Enlightenment, the attainment of nirvana. To deny that here the

Buddha is saying that infinite kindness, compassion, etc. bring Enlightenment is to do violence to the text. This denial however became orthodox at a very early stage. I refer back to the second paragraph of this chapter: I think that systematisers may have falsified the Buddha's views, sacrificing power and beauty of thought in order to build a coherent system.

According to the brahmin ideology to which the Buddha is responding, every significant act, karma, brings its result, but that result is finite; even life in heaven does not last forever. To escape this finitude requires gnosis; then one may join brahman, infinite in space and time. Brahman pervades the entire universe as conscioușness (*cit*).

Here the Buddhist monk is pervading the universe with his consciousness, but it is an ethicised consciousness. In enlarging his mind to be boundless (metaphorically, of course) he is emulating the brahmin gnostic who identifies with universal consciousness – or rather, going one better, showing the brahmin what he really should be doing. His consciousness, moreover, is not a thing, but a process, an activity. It is karma, but not the kind of karma that is finite: that he has transcended. The words 'that' (the finite karma) 'does not remain there' are repeated, for solemn emphasis; I catch here an echo of the Upaniṣadic style, in which weighty conclusions are commonly thus repeated. Having transcended the finitude of normal ('typical') karma, he is fit, like the brahmin gnostic, to join brahman at death. Even the vacillation between the singular and the plural of Brahmā seems to echo the *Bṛhadāraṇyaka Upaniṣad*.

If one thus understands the context, one will see that the joining brahman at death is not to be taken literally; no more than is the Buddha's introductory promise to show the way to the brahma-world. The way to the brahma-world is just Vedāntic language, borrowed from the interlocutor, for the way to nirvana in this life, and by the same token the joining brahma at death is a metaphor for the nirvana which follows the death of an *arahant*. However, this was not understood by the compilers of other *suttas*, let alone by the commentators. The *ceto-vimutti* they took as a metaphor, whereas the joining Brahmā at death they took literally. Thus, though the text clearly says that the kind monk is released, the tradition said that he was reborn at a specific level in the universe, that inhabited by Brahmās. I shall return to the ramifications of this literalism in the next chapter.

We find here the two salient characteristics of the Buddha's theory of *kamma*. Firstly, process substitutes for objects: instead of identifying with universal consciousness one is to think in a certain way; salvation is a matter of *how* one lives, not of *what* one is. Secondly, the process is ethicised: to be totally benevolent is to be liberated.

* * *

I am claiming that a close reading of the *Tevijja Sutta* shows that the Buddha taught that kindness – what Christians tend to call love – was a way to salvation. This claim should be of broad interest for historians of religion. My interpretation of the text has depended on seeing it as an answer to the *Bṛhadāraṇyaka Upaniṣad*.

I think that there is another, less well known, canonical text, which carries much the same message in exactly the same way. This text, SN *sutta* III, 1, 8 = SN I, 75, is so short that I can reproduce it in full. (I omit the repetitions, which are merely a feature of the oral style.)

King Pasenadi had gone to the upper terrace of the palace with Queen Mallikā. Then he said to her, 'To you is there anyone dearer than self?' 'Great king, to me there is no one dearer than self. How about you?' 'To me too, Mallikā, there is no one dearer than self.'

Then when the king had gone down from the terrace he went to the Blessed One. He greeted the Blessed One and sat down to one side, and recounted the conversation to him.

Understanding this matter, the Blessed One thereupon spoke this verse: 'Having traversed all directions in thought, he nowhere found one dearer than self. In this way, for others too the separate self is dear. Therefore one who loves self should not harm others.'

The conversation between the king and queen is surely a reminiscence of the famous conversation in the *Bṛhadāraṇyaka* between the sage Yājñavalkya and his favourite wife Maitreyī. That conversation occurs twice in the Upaniṣad, at II, 4 and IV, 5; the passage relevant for us is the same in both versions. Maitreyī asks her husband to tell her what he knows, knowledge which will make her immortal. He begins his teaching: 'It is not for the love of a husband that a husband is dear, but for the love of self (*ātman*) that a husband is dear. It is not for the love of a wife that a wife is dear, but for the love of self that a wife is dear.' A series of parallel statements leads on to the conclusion that to know the self is to know everything.

In my translations I have used the bare word 'self', which does not sound very idiomatic in English, but this is the best I can do to preserve and highlight an ambiguity in Pali and Sanskrit which is crucial. Pali *atta*, like Sanskrit *ātman*, is the reflexive pronoun, so that the natural English translation of King Pasenadi's question would be 'To you is there anyone dearer than yourself?'; in the reply one would translate with 'myself'; in the Buddha's verse 'himself'; and in the Yājñavalkya's first sentence 'herself'. But the Pali/Sanskrit form does not vary with the person or number of the subject; whose 'self' is in question is understood from the context. It is this invariance of form which makes it particularly easy to hypostatise a Self. Thus in Yājñavalkya's teaching what at first looks like a reflexive pronoun turns out to be the Self, the essence of the universe.

I interpret the Buddha's verse as a rebuttal of Yājñavalkya, half playful and half serious. From Yājñavalkya's premise, or something extremely like it, he draws the opposite conclusion: that one should care for others. Again ethics in place of metaphysics.

A close reading of the verse will buttress this interpretation. The first line, the remark about mentally traversing all directions, links this text to the *Tevijja Sutta.* In the third line is the unusual expression *puthu attā*, which I have translated as 'separate self'. It refers to the common sense view of the individual, the moral agent. But the term seems to allude, by implication, to a contrasting view of self, a 'non-separate self', the Upaniṣadic cosmic Self. That view is not directly mentioned, let alone argued against; the Buddha simply bypasses it.

So here too we see the Buddha reacting to Upaniṣadic teachings by shifting attention away from what the world is, ontology, to how we should behave: morally, and in particular kindly.

This little text does not go so far as to claim that being kind is salvific; this fits the fact that it is not about monks but is addressed to a layman. To us it may seem that a layman can and should be as kind as a monk; but the assumption that to achieve nirvana it is necessary to leave the world seems to me to underlie all the Buddha's teaching. Moreover, because of the tendency to take texts literally, it is debatable whether the *Tevijja Sutta* has had a good influence on the history of Buddhism. Kindness and compassion have been interpreted primarily as mental attitudes, meditative exercises rather than calls to action. This has been noted by observers in many Buddhist cultural settings.

* * *

Whether the Buddha believed in a self is revealed as a pseudo-problem. He certainly believed, above all else, in moral agency; and for many people in the rest of the world that would be an adequate definition of the soul. The Buddha would have accepted the existentialist formulation, 'Je suis mes actes'; but he would not have accepted it in an existentialist spirit, for he was at pains to show the effect of past actions – we might call it character formation – and to stress morality as the foundation of everything worthwhile, both within life and beyond.

III

Metaphor, Allegory, Satire

Summaries of the Buddha's teachings rarely convey how much use he made of simile and metaphor. Many people know that *nirvāṇa/nibbāna* means 'blowing out', but probably few of them know, or perhaps even ask themselves, what is being blown out. The Buddha had a simple, urgent message to convey, and was ingenious in finding ever new terms and analogies by which to convey it. The *suttas* are full of his inventiveness. When he resorted to figurative or other indirect modes of expression, this is called *pariyāya*, literally 'a way round'; it is 'a way of putting things'. The systematised presentation of the doctrine in the *abhidhamma* contrasted itself with teaching by *pariyāya*. The P.E.D., *s.v. pariyāya*, says: 'in Abhidhamma terminology, specifically: *pariyāyena*, the mode of teaching in the Suttanta, *ad hominem*, discursively, applied method, illustrated discourse, figurative language as opposed to the abstract, general statements of Abhidhamma = *nippariyāyena*.'

At the beginning of the previous chapter I raised the question of how accurately the systematisers – the *abhidhamma* and the learned Theravādin tradition – presented the Buddha's thought. In this chapter I shall pursue the same theme, albeit at times rather obliquely, and raise questions about how literally various features of the early texts are to be interpreted, questions to which I myself have in many cases no answers.

Nirvana is part of an extended metaphorical structure which embraces Enlightenment and its opposite. What has to be blown out is the set of three fires: passion (or greed), hatred and delusion. According to tradition, the Buddha introduced the concept of these three fires in his third sermon (Vin I, 34-5 = SN IV, 19). This sermon is known in English as the Fire Sermon, but in Pali it is called the *Āditta-pariyāya*, 'The way of putting things as being on fire'. The sermon begins with the bald and startling statement, 'Everything, O monks, is on fire.' The Buddha then explains what he means by 'everything'. It is all our faculties (the five senses plus the mind), their objects and operations and the feelings they give rise to. All these are on fire with the fires of passion, hatred and delusion.

I have shown in an earlier article (Gombrich, 1990:17-20) that the fires number three because the Buddha was alluding to a set of three fires which the brahmin householder was committed to keeping alight and tending daily, so that they came to symbolise life in the world, life as a family man. This is made crystal clear in a sermon (AN IV, 41-6) in which the Buddha first juxtaposes the three sacrificial fires with the fires of passion, hatred and delusion, and then, with the aid of puns, metaphorically reinterprets the former: the eastern fire, *āhavanīya* in Sanskrit, he says stands for one's parents; the western (*gārhapatya*) fire for one's household and dependents; the southern (*dakṣiṇāgni*) for holy men (renunciates and brahmins) worthy to receive offerings. It is in this sense, he tells a fat brahmin, that a householder should tend the fires: by supporting *people*.

Later generations of Buddhists had no reason to be interested in Vedic brahmins or in the Buddha's debate with them, so the origin of this metaphor was forgotten. So far as I know, it is not to be found in the commentaries. In the Mahāyāna, the metaphor was so thoroughly forgotten that passion, hatred and delusion came to be known as the three poisons.[1] I hope it is not too far-fetched to suggest that this may have contributed to an important development in the Mahāyāna: that it came to separate nirvana from *bodhi*, 'awakening' to the truth, Enlightenment, and to put a lower value on the former (Gombrich, 1992d). Originally nirvana and *bodhi* refer to the same thing; they merely use different metaphors for the experience. But the Mahāyāna tradition separated them and considered that nirvana referred only

[1] Sanskrit *tri-doṣa*. This term is also found in Vasubandhu's *Abhidharmakośabhāṣya* (Takasaki, 1987:144).

to the extinction of craving (= passion and hatred), with the resultant escape from the cycle of rebirth. This interpretation ignores the third fire, delusion: the extinction of delusion is of course in the early texts identical with what can be positively expressed as gnosis, Enlightenment.

Since even the core of the fire metaphor was thus early forgotten by Buddhist tradition, it is not surprising that its extensions were forgotten too. The word *upādāna* has both a concrete and an abstract meaning. In the abstract it means attachment, grasping; in this sense it is much used in Buddhist dogmatics. Concretely, it means that which fuels this process. The P.E.D. *s.v.*: '(lit. that [material] substratum by means of which an active process is kept alive and going), fuel, supply, provision'. So when the context deals with fire it simply means fuel. The five *khandha*, from form to consciousness, are often referred to in the texts as the *upādāna-kkhandhā*, and this is usually translated something like 'the aggregates of grasping'. While not wrong, this translation has lost the metaphor.

In my opinion it is clear that the term *khandha* too was a part of the fire metaphor. I would trace it back to a small *sutta* which has caused a good deal of trouble in the history of Buddhist thought: the sermon about the burden at *Saṃyutta Nikāya Khandha-vagga*, *sutta* 22 = SN III, 25-6. Like most of these short sermons in the *Saṃyutta Nikāya*, this has no narrative context. The Buddha simply begins by saying: 'Monks, I shall teach you the burden, the bearer of the burden, the taking up of the burden and the putting down of the burden.' He is expounding a metaphor. The burden, he says, is what we may call the five *upādāna-kkhandha*; he then names the standard five, from matter to consciousness, calling each an *upādāna-kkhandha*. Each is being metaphorically called a bundle of fuel. The normal fuel was firewood, and we can, if we like, extend the image to being one of the brahmin student (*brahmacārin*), one of whose daily duties was to collect the firewood to feed the sacred fires.

The *sutta* caused trouble because of the next section of the metaphor: the Buddha says that the bearer of the burden is a venerable monk here (*ayaṃ āyasmā*), an individual (*puggala*) with a certain name and clan. His taking up the burden is craving (*taṇhā*) and his laying down the burden is the complete stopping of craving.[2] Later a whole school of Buddhists, the *pudgala-vādin*, took this text as their main authority for claiming that the person was a sixth entity, separate from the five *khandha*, since it was that person, not the five *khandha*, which was subject to craving and so picked the *khandha* up. We can see that this interpretation is nothing but the too literal application of a metaphor, a piece of rather absurd pedantry.

There is a short text a little later in the *Saṃyutta Nikāya*, at SN III, 71, which states that the five *khandha* are on fire (*āditta*), so that one should stop caring for them. I wonder whether this was not the original form of the metaphor of 'being on fire': the experiences of the unenlightened are like five bundles of firewood which are on fire. That would make them very uncomfortable to carry! Indeed, I wonder whether these two short texts, SN III, 25-6 and SN III, 71, were not originally together.

Once one understands that the five processes that constitute our experiences are being compared to burning bundles of firewood, or at least to bundles of firewood to feed the fires of passion, hatred and delusion, this also makes sense of the old terms for the two kinds of nirvana: *sa-upādi-sesa* and *an-upādi-sesa*. As the P.E.D. *s.v. upādi* tells us, *upādi* = *upādāṇa*. The attainment of nirvana during one's life (the only time when it is possible to attain it!) is called *sa-upādi-sesa*, but this does not mean that one still has a residue of grasping – just a little bit of vice! If we follow the metaphor, we understand that at the moment when we extinguish the fires of passion, hatred and delusion we still have the five *khandha*, that which experiences, so we still have a

[2] The metaphor is by no means confined to this text. One of the common epithets for an Enlightened person is *ohita-bhāra*, 'having laid down the burden'; many instances are listed in P.E.D. *s.v.* *arahant* II C. The synonym *panna-bhāra* is used in the same way, e.g. at *Dhammapada* 402, where the commentary (DhA IV, 168) glosses it as *ohita-khandha-bhāro*, 'having laid down the burden of the *khandha*'.

residue (*sesa*) of fuel (*upādi*); however, it is no longer burning. When the five *khandha* cease to exist, i.e., when we die Enlightened, we have no more potential for experience; we have run out of fuel.

This was apparently forgotten at a very early stage. Because of phonetic similarity, *upādi* in this context was changed to *upadhi*. The latter means basis, foundation, and in particular was used to refer to the basis for craving (*taṇhā*). As this made satisfactory sense, no one noticed that there was even a problem with the original terms.

On the other hand, it is surprising that the Mahāyāna forgot the metaphor of the three fires, because the basic idea of the Fire Sermon is preserved in one of the most famous passages in the whole of Mahāyāna literature, the allegory of the burning house in the *Lotus Sūtra* (chapter 3). Here the world is compared to a huge mansion, rickety and rotten, which is on fire while children are heedlessly playing inside; their father has to cajole them to escape from it by promising them fine toys, toys which are punningly compared by the text to the different paths to salvation (*yāna*) which Buddhism offers. The promises serve to get the children – suffering beings – out of the house, but the father – the Buddha – only in fact gives the biggest kind of toy, the Great Vehicle (*Mahā-yāna*). This is called his skill in means. The text's use of metaphor and punning is very much in the tradition of the Buddha's style of argument as found in the Pali Canon; but I believe that the application of the concept 'skill in means' to saying something untrue, albeit with the noblest motives, is an innovation. Let me hasten to add that I do not intend this observation to be pejorative. My own ethical opinion is that lying is justified if it achieves a great good, such as saving life. I am making a factual historical point about how Buddhist doctrine developed.

The *Lotus Sūtra* has made a story out of the fire metaphor in the Fire Sermon, and so moved it onto the plane of allegory. I think that the same thing had been done much earlier: in the very passage in the *Mahāvagga* of the *Vinaya Khandhaka* in which the

Fire Sermon is presented in a narrative context. The Buddha preaches that sermon to a thousand newly-converted brahmin fire-worshippers, and indeed at the end of it all of them are said to achieve Enlightenment. This comes as the culmination to what is by the standards of these texts a very long episode, ten pages of Pali (Vin I, 24-34) in the standard edition. In this episode the Buddha seems, if I may say so, to behave in a rather strange manner. There are texts (e.g., DN I, 213) in which he says that he loathes the display of miracles. But here he performs a whole series of them. He has come upon three brahmin ascetics, all of the Kassapa lineage (*gotra*),[3] who between them have a thousand disciples. They are fire-worshippers, and evidently keep the sacred fire (the narrative says nothing of there being three) in a separate little fire-house. The Buddha asks to spend the night in Uruvela Kassapa's fire-house. The ascetic warns him that there is a *nāga*, a supernatural cobra, living in there who may burn him up. The Buddha goes in and successfully vies with the *nāga* in heating himself up, though of course he does not hurt him. The whole fire-house seems to be on fire (*āditta*) because of the heat the two of them generate. Moreover, the Buddha's flames come in five colours. Kassapa is impressed by this miracle, but not yet sufficiently impressed to be converted. The Buddha then performs several more miracles. Not all of them have to do with fire, but the last one does, and the brahmins finally throw away their fire-worshipping gear (*aggihutta-missaṃ*) and convert (p. 33). It is at this point that the narrative places the Fire Sermon.

If one takes this narrative literally, one has to ask oneself why the Buddha did not adopt his usual tactic for converting people, namely preaching to them. Instead he resorted to a series of displays which normally he regarded as undignified at best. When the monk Piṇḍola Bhāradvāja has displayed his power of levitation before a crowd, in answer to a challenge, the Buddha

[3] A *gotra* is an exogamous patrilineal descent group.

compares his action to a woman displaying her genitals in public (Vin II, 112). But if one takes the point of view of the compiler of the text, the whole story is ancillary to the Fire Sermon, which has to come as its climax, and to insert a sermon earlier would weaken its impact.

I recounted in chapter 1 how this text begins with claims that the Buddha is a (true) brahmin, claims which are followed by an allegorical depiction of the Buddha's superiority to Brahmā, the god who personifies the brahmins' essence.[4] Here the same theme is carried further: the brahmins' religious practice is metaphorically presented as the epitome of what is wrong with life. The Buddha rejects it not because he is somehow inadequate, e.g., not qualified by birth to perform the fire rituals, for he demonstrates that he has all the power of the fire-worshippers and more; he rejects it because it is the antithesis of what is truly desirable.

It is unlikely to be mere coincidence that in the *āryā* verses[5] describing the contest of heat, at the point when multi-coloured flames come from the Buddha's body (p. 25), he is called Aṅgirasa. The Buddha is called Aṅgirasa or Aṅgīrasa several times in the Pali Canon.[6] Āṅgirasa is a Vedic *gotra*, and it is by virtue of being a Gautama, says Brough, that he is so addressed (Brough, 1953:xv). In the *Ṛg Veda*, however, Aṅgīras is a class of supermen, standing between men and gods, and Agni, the personification of fire, is the first and foremost Aṅgīras (RV I, 31, 1). In other texts too the Buddha is called Aṅgīrasa when he

[4] Almost the same passage about Brahmā's inviting the Buddha to preach appears twice in the *Sutta Piṭaka*. At MN I, 168-9, in the *Ariya-pariyesana Sutta*, the Buddha does not make Brahmā Sahampati (as he is called here and in the *Vinaya*) ask three times, but agrees because of his compassion (*sattesu kāruññataṃ paṭicca*). At DN II, 36-40 the identical episode is recounted about the former Buddha Vipassi; here the invitation to preach is given by Mahā Brahmā. In this last version, Mahā Brahmā reappears in order to persuade Vipassi to send out the first sixty monks as missionaries.

[5] They were not recognised as verses by Oldenberg, but see Alsdorf, 1968:298ff. *Āryā* is a metre.

[6] See D.P.P.N. *s.v.*. All references there given in footnote 1 are to verse passages.

is said to shine very brilliantly: at SN I, 196 he outshines the world; at AN III, 239 (= J I, 116) he shines and glows like the sun. So in this passage he is virtually impersonating Agni, the brahmins' fire god. This looks less like a debate than a takeover bid.

* * *

There is another contest or debate going on which we cannot entirely piece together: a contest with *nāga* worship. This is the second passage in the *Mahāvagga* narrative where the Buddha seems to be confronting the *nāgas*. In the first case the relationship is more cooperative, just as the relationship with Brahmā is cooperative. Shortly after his Enlightenment, the Buddha is sitting in the bliss of meditation when a great storm arises (Vin I, 3). To protect him, the *nāga* king Mucalinda comes and wraps his coils round the Buddha and spreads his hood over the Buddha's head.[7] When the storm has passed, he takes the form of a young brahmin and renders homage to the Buddha. He does not say anything, and we cannot tell why he takes human form; but this episode too has the air of being an allegory of religious rivalry.

There is epigraphic and archaeological evidence for the worship of *nāgas* in shrines and temples (Härtel, 1993:426-7). Härtel has excavated a *nāga* temple at Sonkh, near Mathurā, which he dates to the Kuṣāṇa period. He considers that the area round Rājagṛha had a lot of *nāga* worship. A structure at Rājagṛha known as Maṇiyār Maṭha has been securely identified by excavators as a *nāga* shrine; its oldest strata are dated to the second or first century B.C..[8] Though this is well after the time of the Buddha, it

[7] In Jaina iconography the last Jina before Mahāvīra, Pārśvanātha, is similarly shown seated with his head protected by a seven-headed cobra (Fischer & Jain, 1974: plates 11, 21, 27).

[8] H. K. Prasad (1960:133) mentions the Mucalinda episode in connection with the *nāga* cult in Bihar, and cites others who have done so, but he does not posit religious rivalry.

is about as old as the evidence for any Indian shrine or temple, so it seems reasonable to extrapolate by projecting the cult back a couple of centuries to his day.

The narrative we have been discussing occurs at the beginning of the book which gives the rules for monastic communal life, the *Vinaya Khandhaka*. More specifically, it occurs at the beginning of the first chapter, the main topic of which is the rules for ordination. Among these is the rule that an animal may not be ordained; if it has been, it is to be unfrocked. There is an anecdote to explain how each rule came to be made. In this case the story (Vin I, 86-8) is that a *nāga* was fed up with being a *nāga* and pondered how it could quickly become human. To this end it took human form and got itself ordained. But when it relaxed and fell asleep it filled up its cell so that its coils came out of the window. The neighbouring monk saw this and shrieked. The Buddha then said to the *nāga* that *nāgas* did not have the capacity to progress in his doctrine and discipline; he should go and observe the *uposatha* days (quarter days of the lunar month) like a good layman and that way would soon become a human. The *nāga* went away crying, while the Buddha told the monks that *nāgas* were bound to reveal their nature as *nāgas* on two occasions: when they had sex and when they relaxed and fell asleep.

A further curious fact is that in Sri Lanka candidates for the higher ordination (*upasampadā*) are dressed in elegant lay clothes with a cloth so arranged over their heads as to resemble a cobra's hood, and are called '*nāga*'. I have often asked why, and been offered a bewildering variety of explanations, all of which have struck me as composed *ad hoc*.

The word *nāga* in Sanskrit and Pali has three distinct meanings: supernatural cobra (the meaning discussed so far), elephant, and ironwood tree. At the seminar, Mr Sumana Ratnayaka quoted a saying that the *nāga* is the greatest among trees, among serpents, and among the laity. He added that the *nāga* was a symbol of wealth, like the Chinese dragon. This seems to take the question of the ordination candidate a step further, though it remains unclear how this symbolism arose.

There are occasions when important monks are referred to as *mahānāga* (e.g. MN I, 32; MN I, 151).[9] This certainly shows that in the Pali texts *nāga* when applied to humans did not denote lay status.

Similarly, at *Sutta-nipāta* verse 518 it is asked on what grounds four epithets are applied: *brāhmaṇa*, *samaṇa* ('renunciate'), *nhātaka* (literally: 'bathed'; a high brahminical ritual status); *nāga*. All four answers (in the following verses) play upon words and provide justification for applying these terms to an Enlightened person metaphorically. He is called *nāga* because he commits no *āgu*, 'offence'. The person so called is here referred to as *tādi*, 'like that'; later this came to be considered an epithet only of a Buddha, but here I think it can refer more broadly to any Enlightened person.

If the same game is here being played with all four words – and that seems a reasonable supposition – we can surmise that just as Buddhism was competing with brahminism and with other groups of renunciates, it was competing with *nāga* worship,[10] and using the same technique of appropriating the opponent's terms and infusing them with a new meaning. If that is so, it could be the root of the Sinhalese ordination custom: the Buddhists are saying to the *nāga* worshippers, 'Our *nāgas* are better than

[9] On MN I, 32 Buddhaghosa comments that the two chief disciples, Sāriputta and Moggallāna, have this epithet; but at MN I, 151 it is applied also to Puṇṇa Mantāṇiputta. The term is explained by the etymology at *Sutta-nipāta* 522 (see next paragraph) and others on similar lines, not as a metaphor (*Papañca-sūdanī* I, 153).

[10] At first blush it might appear that my conclusion was anticipated long ago by James Fergusson in *Tree and Serpent Worship* (Fergusson, 1873). He thought that the aboriginal inhabitants of India were snake-worshippers (see esp. pp. 67, 248), that the Aryan brahmins rejected the cult and 'relegated' their worshippers, imaginatively identified with the snakes they worshipped, 'to their infernal regions' (p. 248), that the Buddha rejected serpent worship himself (p. 244), but that it came back to influence Buddhism, as proved by the name Nāgārjuna. However, even the slight extent to which this theory resembles mine – and it traces a unilinear development, with no notion of debate – is coincidence, for Fergusson had no access to or knowledge of any Pali canonical text.

yours.' In that case the saying quoted by Mr Ratnayaka may have been invented to account for the custom when its origin had been forgotten.

* * *

Without attempting to analyse the text exhaustively, I have argued that much of the narrative telling what the Buddha did in the days and weeks following his Enlightenment is allegorical in origin; and I suspect that one could push this argument even further. The same goes for his biography up to the Enlightenment. Others have noticed this before me, so I shall not dwell on it. The stress on the luxury in which the future Buddha was brought up serves to emphasise his mature rejection of worldly goods. His being shielded from all knowledge of old age, sickness and death symbolises the way in which we turn a blind eye to the unpleasant facts of existence, and heightens the impact of the prince's encounter with the four 'signs' or omens (*pubba nimitta*): the story of how on his way to the pleasure grounds he successively encounters an aged man, an ill man, a corpse, and a tranquil ascetic who seems to offer the solution. Nowhere in the Canon is this story told of Siddhattha Gotama, nor does even the name Siddhattha occur in the Canon. Siddhattha means 'fulfiller of purpose'. Normally a father would give this name to his son referring to the fact that it is every man's duty to perpetuate his line by having a son. But in this case no doubt the reference is to the Buddha's higher purpose. There is an added irony in the story when it is told of Siddhattha: that on the day when he has confronted decay and death, he himself becomes the father of a son – whom he leaves behind with all the other usual human comforts and achievements.

In the Canon this story is not told of Siddhattha, and the birth of the son is omitted. The story of the four encounters is told of Vipassi, six Buddhas back (DN II, 21-9). According to this text, the *Mahâpadāna Sutta*, the early lives (and to some extent the later lives) of all Buddhas follow a very similar pattern, and the five Buddhas between Vipassi and Gotama will have experienced the same encounters. I have elsewhere (Gombrich, 1980) published a theory about the origin of the doctrine of former Buddhas, and, separately, a theory about why at first there is a set of seven (Gombrich, 1992c). I do not think that the content of the *Mahâpadāna Sutta* can go back to the time of the Buddha. Its allegorical character strikes me as very like that of the introduction to the *Vinaya Khandhaka*. This takes one back to Frauwallner's theory (originally proposed by Finot) that there was a single biography of the Buddha, composed to frame an account of how the *Vinaya* rules came into being (Frauwallner 1956: 42-3; 130-1; 153-4). It would have been composed a couple of generations after the Buddha's death;[11] and parts of it were in verse.

To hold this theory is not to deny that there were older traditions about the Buddha's life which could go back to the Buddha's contemporaries. Even they could well have composed accounts which would not correspond to our idea of the literal truth. An interesting and perhaps insoluble problem is posed by the pair of poems which begins the third book of the *Sutta-nipāta*, the *Mahā Vagga*. The first poem is the *Pabbajjā Sutta*. It tells how after leaving home (*pabbajjā*) the Buddha met King Bimbisāra, who invited him to stay as an honoured guest. (The poem calls him the Buddha (v.408) even though he was not yet Enlightened.) It begins (v.405): 'I shall proclaim the leaving home: how the visionary left home; how on consideration he decided for leaving home.' Although the Buddha sometimes refers to himself in the third person, this sounds very much as if the poem is frankly the work of a follower.

[11] Frauwallner's dating of the work to 'the first half of the 4th century B.C.' (p. 131) and 'about 100 years after the Nirvana' (p. 153) rests on dating the Buddha's death to c.483 B.C., and accepting that the second council took place just 100 years later. Since I have shown that the Buddha probably died in the last decade of the fifth century B.C. (Gombrich, 1992a) and that the second council was very roughly 65 years later, this takes us to the third quarter of the 4th century B.C..

By contrast, however, the next poem, the *Padhāna Sutta* ('Poem on Exertion'), begins (v.425): 'While I was exerting myself ....' (hence the title). The first words are *tam maṃ*, literally 'that me'. *Taṃ* is an anaphoric pronoun; in other words, it picks up the subject of the previous sentence. The previous sentence, of course, is the last line of the *Pabbajjā Sutta*. That is the end of the Buddha's speech declining King Bimbisāra's invitation: 'I shall go for exertion; in that my mind delights.' Both the anaphoric pronoun and the repetition of 'exertion' (with the same root but in different grammatical form) show that originally the two poems were one. Yet if the *Padhāna Sutta* is taken in isolation, it does sound as if it were a piece of narration in the first person. The commentary ascribes the *Pabbajjā Sutta* to Ānanda and the *Padhāna Sutta* to the Buddha (*Paramattha-jotikā* II, 2, p. 386), but against the above argument for the original unity of the two poems that carries no weight with me.

This is relevant to the theme of allegory, for the *Padhāna Sutta* tells the story of the Buddha's Enlightenment in entirely allegorical terms, as a battle against Māra, the personification of death. In fact it may be the earliest text to tell of this episode. But there is an interesting discrepancy between this account and the later story. The story which every Buddhist knows is that the Buddha tried to reach Enlightenment by extreme asceticism, but only reached his goal on realising that that was the wrong way and he should take the middle path between asceticism and indulgence. In the accepted version, he takes his first decent meal for years before spending the night on which he overcomes Māra and wins through to Enlightenment.

In this poem, however, Māra is tempting the Buddha to give up his asceticism, to which the Buddha defiantly replies (v.434) that the more his flesh wastes away the calmer his mind becomes and the more stable his awareness, concentration and understanding. That is the opposite of the first sermon's exhortation to follow the middle path, the message allegorised in the accepted version.[12] At first sight it seems ironic that Māra, Death, is inviting the Buddha to live (v.427: *jīva bho, jīvitaṃ seyyo*); but for Buddhists Māra at the same time represents desire, and the life he is urging is life in the world, performing the fire sacrifice (*aggihutta*). He has an army of which the first force is sensual desires (*kāmā*); there seem to be about ten forces, consisting of a variety of desires and moral temptations, ending with boasting and disparaging others. Thus the allegory shows that normal life is really death – repeated death.

That is orthodox enough. But (to digress briefly from allegory) the depiction of the Buddha as defeating Māra by dint of mortifying the flesh is anything but orthodox. It is at least as good an example as any of those adduced by Professor Bronkhorst[13] of what he calls Jain influence, in this case the view that it is asceticism which brings release from the cycle of rebirth. I see it as part – the losing side – of a debate among Buddhists, which may at the same time (we cannot tell) have been a debate with non-Buddhists. I see this text as motivated by a spirit similar to that which composed the *Mahā Sīhanāda Sutta* (MN *sutta* 12). There the Buddha claims that he performed austerities more extreme than anyone, for example that he slept on human bones in cemeteries and that he would crawl into cowpens to eat the cowdung, and that he consumed his own faeces and urine so long as he was still producing any (MN I, 79). I have the impression that later Buddhists have been chary of quoting this passage. Unlike the *Padhāna Sutta*, the *Mahā Sīhanāda Sutta*

[12] The commentary resorts to the desperate explanation (p. 391) that between two verses (441 and 442) there is a long time gap. It alleges that after the Buddha has spoken verse 441 Māra quietly leaves. The Buddha then sees that his austerities are getting him nowhere, accepts food from Sujātā and settles down under the Bo tree, determined to win Enlightenment. Māra now returns with his army and the battle between them takes place as in the standard account. At this point the Buddha utters verse 442. All that this explanation proves is that the poem posed a real problem to the systematisers.

[13] Cf. p. 19 above.

does not claim that these practices led to Enlightenment; but on the other hand the Buddha does not say in the latter text that he was wrong to do them, only that they were ineffective (MN I, 81). On the contrary, he seems to be boasting. The author of the text is saying, as it were: 'Anything your guru can do, ours has done better.'

It is very hard to tell how seriously one is supposed to take Māra. In fact I suppose that there is no one answer to this: that different authors and compilers had different opinions and attitudes. Since all the world around us, including the hells beneath us and the heavens of the gods (*deva*) above us, are within the plane of desire (*kāmâvacara*), Māra is allegorically said to reside in the highest of those heavens, so that he presides over the world of which human beings are at the centre and holds it in his grasp; this is graphically depicted in Tibetan pictures of the wheel of life, in which this world is shown in the grip of a devouring demon. But the Pali texts tend to treat Māras more lightly – just like Brahmā, though Māra begins as a single personification, he comes to be multiplied. Thus in the *sutta* of *The Rebuke to Māra* (*Māra-tajjaniya Sutta*, MN *sutta* 50) the elder Moggallāna feels a weight in his belly as if he had been eating beans. On reflection he realises that the weight is Māra, and he orders him to come out, or it will be the worse for him. At first Māra demurs, thinking, 'Even his teacher would not recognise me quickly, so how can his disciple recognise me?' But when he realises that he has truly been spotted he comes out from the elder's mouth and stays at the door,[14] presumably biding his time. The elder says, 'Don't think I can't see you, wicked one; you're right here at the door. Once I was a Māra called Dūsī (Corrupter), and I had a sister called Kāḷī, and you were her son, so you were my nephew.' He goes on to recount how at that time

[14] P.E.D.. *s.v. paccaggaḷa* says that Māra stuck in his throat, but that contradicts the previous phrase, that he came out of his mouth (p. 333). The commentary (MA II, 416) has this right.

he as Dūsī harassed the Buddha Kakusandha, as a result of which he ended up broiling in hell. Presumably the point of Moggallāna's claiming to have been Māra's uncle is to assert his authority over him.[15] That Māra was the son of Kāḷī I shall return to in my last chapter. This anecdote follows the standard pattern of exorcism (even if self-exorcism is unusual); note the importance of knowing the name of the possessing spirit. It reduces Māra to the level of a commonplace incubus, and even seems to make fun of him.

There is similar humour about Māra at the end of the *Padhāna Sutta.* Māra says he has been following the Buddha for seven years, awaiting his chance. He is compared to a crow circling a stone which looks like a lump of fat. When he finds it is just a stone he leaves. The *vīṇā* falls from Māra's armpit – we were not previously told that he was carrying a musical instrument – and, despondent, he disappears (*tato so dummano yakkho tatth' ev' antaradhāyatha*). We must bear in mind that Māra, there called Mṛtyu, figures in the Brāhmaṇas as personified Death; there of course he is taken seriously. Satirizing Māra was therefore much like satirizing Brahmā. I suspect that in both cases the original spirit of the satire may have been rather light-hearted, even when it made serious points.

* * *

There can be no doubt that the Buddha used allegory satirically. I have published analyses (Gombrich, 1990, 1992b) of two passages in the Pali Canon, one short and one long, which make fun of brahminical accounts of how the world began. The short one is about Brahmā. In one of the accounts of the creation in the *Bṛhadāraṇyaka Upaniṣad* (1, 4, 1-3), in the beginning there was only *ātman* in human form. I have explained in chapter 2 that *ātman* and *brahman* in the Upaniṣad are synonymous at the

[15] I am grateful to my wife, Sanjukta Gupta, for explaining this to me.

cosmic level, and that *brahman* (neuter) in turn may be personified as Brahmā (masculine). Here it is the *ātman* which is being personified, and as the word is already masculine no change of gender is required. 'He was afraid. So a person alone is afraid. He considered: since nothing but me exists, what am I afraid of? So his fear went away, for it is of something else that one is afraid. He really had no fun. So a person alone has no fun. He wanted another person. He was as big as a man and a woman in embrace, so he split that very self of his into two, so that husband and wife came into being.'

In the Buddhist passage, which occurs several times in the Canon (e.g. DN I, 17-18), the world is assumed to be eternal but to go through cycles of destruction and re-formation. We can say provisionally that the destruction takes place below the level of some very rarefied heavens, well above the plane of desire, and that while nothing exists lower down, transmigrating beings are reborn in those very high heavens. But existence in all heavens, however high and rarefied, is of course temporary. When it is time for a new world-cycle (*vivaṭṭa-kalpa*), the celestial palace which Brahmā occupies reappears, empty. In due course, a being whose life span or merit has been exhausted dies in the higher heaven and is reborn in that palace – so he is reborn as Brahmā. After he has been there alone for a long time he gets frightened and feels he is having no fun, so he wishes that other beings would come to exist in the mode that he does. Simply in the course of nature, other beings too leave the higher heaven and are reborn alongside Brahmā. Then he nourishes the delusion that they are there because of his wish, and fancies himself an omnipotent creator.

The long passage in the Pali Canon which makes fun of brahminical cosmogony is the *Aggañña Sutta* (DN *sutta* xxvii) (see Gombrich, 1992b for details). The whole story of the origin of society, which forms the bulk of the text, is a parody of brahminical texts, especially the Ṛg Vedic 'Hymn of Creation' (RV X, 129) and the cosmogony at BĀU 1, 2. The formation of the earth at the beginning of a world-cycle, its population by beings, their gradual social differentiation, the origins of sex and property, and finally the invention of kingship and the creation of the four brahminical *varna* (social classes) – all are a parodistic re-working of brahminical speculations, and at the same time an allegory of the malign workings of desire.

This is no minor matter for the history of the Buddhist view of the world. Strictly speaking, the *Aggañña Sutta* is not a cosmogony, since for Buddhists an absolute beginning is inconceivable (SN II,178ff.); but it explains how the world came into being this time round, so with this caveat I shall use the word. Buddhists have since the earliest times taken it seriously as an account of the origins of society and kingship, and even traced the Buddha's own royal origins back to Mahā-sammata, the person chosen to be the first king; they have interpreted the word as a proper name, though it originally meant 'agreed to be great'. But now we see that the Buddha never intended to propound a cosmogony.

If we take a close look at the *Aggañña Sutta*, there are considerable incoherencies if it is taken seriously as an explanatory account – though once it is perceived to be a parody these inconsistencies are of no account. Already in the Canon this text provided part of the basis of Buddhist cosmology, and these inconsistencies provided the systematisers with problems, some of which were never properly solved. I mentioned above that we could 'provisionally' say that the world is periodically destroyed below a certain very high level; and this assumption was the essential background to the humorous attack on the idea that Brahmā created the world. The resultant cosmology, with complicated cycles of destruction up to various levels, is meticulously worked out in the *Visuddhi-magga* (XII, paras. 30ff. = pp. 349ff.).[16] But a moment's reflection will show that this can hardly fit the basic Buddhist theory of how the law of karma operates. In order to be reborn so high in the universe, above

[16] Ed. Warren & Kosambi, Harvard 1950.

even Brahmā and far above the plane of desire, one must have overcome desire in one's previous life and be spiritually so advanced that one is unlikely to come back to earth even once, let alone to recommence a long series of lowly lives. The theory could, with a little squeezing, be made to allow a few such cases; but it could not allow for every single karmic continuum simultaneously to result in such an elevated rebirth, only to be followed by mass relapse.

* * *

The main interest of cosmology for Buddhists is to specify the states in which one may be reborn. The final Theravādin map of the cosmos can be said to contain two models, one encapsulated within the other. The smaller one corresponds to the five (or six) *gati*, the states in which one may be reborn *grosso modo* according to the quality of one's karma. In this model human beings are more or less in the middle, at least in spatial terms. Above them are the heavens of the gods (divided into six levels). At the same level as human beings, though less well off, are animals and ghosts. There is sometimes said to be a layer of anti-gods (*asura*) just beneath the earth, but this inheritance from Vedic cosmology has no lasting importance in Buddhism. Below the earth are many hells full of suffering hell-beings.

All this, as mentioned above, is the plane of desire (*kāmâvacara*). The kind of karma that gets you there is what in chapter 2 I called 'typical' karma. But there is also the question, for Buddhists, of what happens to people who have made great spiritual progress in meditation but not yet quite attained nirvana. Meditation had been classified into many levels, of which all but the very lowest implied transcendence of this world of desire; what happened if one died while within such a state? What happened, in other words, to those who were now living entirely the life of the mind – whose karma was purely 'dogmatic', as I have put it?

At the same time, the systematisers wanted to take on board the brahminical concept that Brahmā was on a higher plane than the mere gods (*deva*). However, they also wanted to trump Brahmā and claim that his world was not the highest: the Buddhists had a higher one.

The result of all this was that in the full map of the cosmos, the plane of desire is only the bottom third of a tri-partite structure. Above that is the plane of form (*rūpâvacara*), which corresponds to the Brahma worlds – for, like Brahmā, the Brahma-world became multiplied. One source of this particular cosmic proliferation we have in fact been examining: there had to be a higher level in which Brahmā had been born before he got that false notion that he was a creator, but that could not be one of the specifically Buddhist levels at the very top, because from those there is no falling back. These Buddhist levels together constitute the plane of no form (*arūpâvacara*); beings in them have no bodies but only minds in states of meditation so high that their attainment of nirvana from that position is assured.

It might be possible, with sufficient research, to trace the origin of every level in this final elaborate scheme. I have not done that research; and I suspect that some of the details might prove rather tedious reading. However, I would like to give an example of how literalism was responsible for creating the cosmology.

In chapter 2 I traced the origin of the four states of mind which came to be known as 'living with brahman' (*brahma-vihāra*). I showed there that originally these were said to be salvific; and that the metaphor of living with (and attaining) brahman arose from that context. However, most of the many passages in which the *brahma-vihāra* are described in the Canon[17] match them up to cosmology in a literal fashion and say that they result in rebirth in

[17] Many of them are listed in Barbara Stoler Miller 1979:218, fn. 1. Miller noted (p. 210): 'It is a well-documented characteristic of early Buddhism that many of its terms and practices are reinterpretations of Brahmanic terms and ritual practices.' But unfortunately I think she missed the specific point here.

the Brahma-world. I cite as typical the *Mahā Govinda Sutta* (DN *sutta* xix). In this text, the Buddha in a former life was a brahmin chaplain called Govinda. In the end he renounced the world with many followers, and practised and taught the four *brahma-vihāra* (DN II, 250).[18] Those who understood his teaching completely were reborn in the brahma-world. Those who did not understand it perfectly were variously reborn, evidently according to the degree of their understanding, in the six worlds of the gods (i.e., heavens), from the highest to the lowest. Those who did least well were reborn as *gandharva*, a kind of semi-divine celestial musician. The text concludes by saying explicitly that that kind of religious life could not bring people beyond rebirth in the world of Brahmā.

Buddhaghosa hardly discusses the *brahma-vihāra* in his commentary on the *Tevijja Sutta* because he says (DA II, 405) that it is all in the *Visuddhi-magga* (where chapter IX is devoted to the *brahma-vihāra*). It is however interesting to see his comment (DA II, 406) on the text's statement that in that condition no finite karma remains. 'What is called finite karma is said to be on the plane of desire; what is called boundless karma is on the planes of form and no form.' He goes on to explain that karma on the planes of form and no form leaves no space for the lower kind of karma, so that it is crowded out and cannot come to fruition, just as a flood pervades and subsumes a small quantity of water. Not only has he lost the original metaphorical structure, as I have already pointed out. He has reified the ethical teaching into a hierarchic cosmology. His reification has even gone a stage further than that: karma is conceived of in spatial terms, so that one kind (my 'dogmatic' karma) leaves no room for another (my 'typical' karma).

[18] The compiler of this text was evidently in agreement with Barbara Stoler Miller and other scholars who have suspected that the *brahma-vihāra* were of brahminical pre-Buddhist origin (see previous footnote)!

Even within the Canon, the *brahma-vihāra* are treated inconsistently. At SN V, 119-121 the four states are hierarchised, with equanimity top. They are matched to numbers 3 to 6 of the set of eight meditative states called *vimokkhā*, 'releases' (on which see chapter 4). So kindness, if practised to perfection, may take one as high as the state labelled 'auspicious' (*subha*); compassion to infinite space; sympathetic joy to infinite consciousness; and equanimity to infinite nothingness. In cosmological terms, the 'auspicious' state is above Brahmā, high up in the plane of form, but the other three are higher, at the lower reaches of the plane of no form.

At the end of his treatment of the *brahma-vihāra* in *Visuddhimagga* IX (pp. 269-70), Buddhaghosa accepts this last version of how high these states can get you. However, he does seem to feel that this schema under-values the *brahma-vihāra*; for in the final paragraph (124) he adds that these four states of mind bring to fulfilment all the Ten Perfections (*dasa pāramī*) and all the other sets of qualities particularly associated with Buddhas: the ten powers (*dasa balāni*), the four kinds of confidence (*vesārajja*), the six kinds of knowledge not shared by disciples (*asādhāraṇa-ñāṇa*) and the eighteen separate states of the Enlightened (*Buddha-dhamma-ppabheda*). This suggests to me that the spirit of a religion may survive even when literalist litterati have lost the point.

* * *

I have said that the higher levels of the cosmology were posited to correspond to meditative states, because of the need to posit suitable rebirths for those who died while in those states. But that is certainly not the whole story. There was a much bigger and more interesting problem: if people realised certain states, surely those states must exist? To put it in our terms, surely these subjective states had some objective correlate?

To explain the problem more clearly, let me refer back to chapter 2. I pointed out that in the Vedānta ontology and epistemology were merged, so that to be wholly and exclusively aware of brahman was at the same time to *be* brahman. (From our worldly angle it seems to be to *become* brahman, but that is ultimately incorrect, because one cannot become what one is already.)

The origins of this idea seem to lie in a theory of sense perception in which the grasping hand supplies a dominant analogy. It takes the shape of what it apprehends. Vision was similarly explained: the eye sends out some kind of ray which takes the shape of what we see and comes back with it. Similarly thought: a thought conforms to its object. This idea is encapsulated in the term *tan-mayatā*, 'consisting of that': that the thought of the gnostic or meditator becomes con-substantial with the thing realised.

In chapter 2 I emphasised that the Buddha did not reify consciousness and never confused epistemology with ontology – at least, at the philosophical level. This qualification refers to the fact that it is still quite obscure to me how the Buddha understood what we call the imagination, and to what extent he thought that mental images exist outside our minds. In looking at this question, however, I remain committed to the doubts I expressed at the beginning of chapter 2: I do not assume *a priori* that the Buddha had a worked out or consistent position on these questions.

If the Buddha or the early Buddhists thought that the subjective thoughts of wise men – I wish to leave aside the problem of possible error or delusion – had objective correlates, they were under the influence of the older idea of correspondence between the microcosm and the macrocosm. Another aspect of this complex of ideas which seems to me to be crucial is conceptions of time.

In a lecture I gave in January 1991 (Gombrich, 1993a) I explained that Buddhists in the early texts (and perhaps still, in certain contexts) have two quite different concepts of time, which are held simultaneously. Cosmic time is, strictly speaking, infinite, since the universe has neither beginning nor end; but in effect it is cyclical, since patterns of events endlesssly recur in predictable (and partly predicted) fashion. On the other hand, we individuals create our experience of time by our own mental activity; once that stops, as it does when we have abolished greed, hatred and delusion, we have no more experience of time.

This dual structure, like so much else in early Buddhism, can best be explained by reference to the brahminical culture which constituted its ideological background, to the speculations about Vedic sacrifice. On the one hand, this speculation embodied cosmology with its mythic time scheme; on the other, it discussed what the sacrificer was achieving by his sacrifice. 'Here came the idea that it was only by incessant attention to the correct maintenance of the cosmic cycle by sacrificial action that a man could produce and order a sequence of time in which to live. For Brahmanical thinking, time and continuity were not simply and deterministically given to man: rather, they are the result of a constant effort at prolongation, a constant pushing forward of life supported by the magical power of sacrifice.' (Collins, 1982:42) Cosmic and personal time were fused in the brahminical theory of sacrifice by the mystical identification of the sacrificer with Prajāpati, the creator god who at the same time embodied the universe. The Buddha, however, denied the validity of sacrifice and argued against (even ridiculed) the identification of the individual with the universe (microcosm with macrocosm); thus he left nothing to hold together the two concepts of time. Though Buddhists reconceptualised the spatial organisation of the universe to make it homologous with their scheme of spiritual progress, no such link was forged between cosmic time and time as we can experience it: the two topics are henceforward unconnected.[19]

After writing the above, I was delighted to come across the following in Mumford's book *Himalayan Dialogue*. In a section headed 'Three layers of temporal identity' (Mumford, 1989:16),

[19] The above paragraph is reproduced from Gombrich, 1993a:150.

he expounds a theory of Mikhail Bakhtin, according to which there are three ways of experiencing time which form a historical sequence. In the first: 'Personal identity is relational, defined in terms of connections between persons and the landmarks of local space. The sense of time in the individual is in harmony with cycles of nature.' In the second: '*The individual life sequence* is a new feeling of interior time, "sealed-off" from other subjectivities. It promotes a directional identity of "individual becoming" that seeks extrication from the world matrix, as in Christian or Buddhist religious destinies and economic individualism. The result is a bifurcation of personal time and world time.' The third stage 'unites the personal sense of time with historical consciousness': we see ourselves as living in history.

Whether or not this is universally true, it certainly seems to me to give a correct and useful account of the relation between the early Buddhist view of time and what must have been generally prevalent in the environment. We note however that the brahmin intellectuals were subtler than Bakhtin gives them credit for, and did try to integrate personal and world time, though in a far from modern manner.

If Mumford, Bakhtin and I are correct, the implication of this would point in the same direction as chapter 2: that the Buddha was not really interested in what existed 'out there'. But I am by no means content to leave the question at that. Though I can do little more than raise the question, there are interesting indications that the Buddha's presuppositions about the macrocosm were very different from ours, and worth studying if for that reason alone.

Even thus, I may have put the question inappropriately. We may ask, for example, whether the Buddha literally believed in the existence of gods or heavens. But is it sure that he would have understood what we mean by 'literally'? G.E.R. Lloyd has shown that one of the foundations of science is the distinction between the literal and the metaphorical, and that it was Aristotle who first insisted on this: '... it is not until Aristotle that we encounter a pair of terms to express the contrast between, on the one hand, a word used strictly or properly (*kuriōs*), and, on the other, its transferred application to another domain. The original or primary sense of *metaphora* in Greek is, approximately, just that, namely transfer ....' Plato warned of the dangers of metaphor and analogy in argument. 'But in Aristotle the negative evaluation, indeed the outright condemnation, of what he calls metaphora in prominent contexts both in his logic and in his natural philosophy are even more clearly marked.' He said (*Topics,* 139b34f) that 'every metaphorical expression is obscure' (Lloyd, 1990:20-1).

I suspect that in describing meditative states the boundary between the literal and the metaphorical is in any case impossible to draw. Then whether a description of a psychological state, a microcosm, is to be taken as literally applicable to the macrocosm or only metaphorically so may be a very hard question to answer.

Let me illustrate the kind of passage I am referring to. I have in chapter 2 discussed the riddle in the *Kevaddha Sutta* which begins, 'Where do earth, water, fire and wind find no footing?' This question is said by the Buddha to occur one day to a monk (DN I, 215). Thereupon, the Buddha relates, the monk enters such a state of concentration (*samādhi*) that the path leading to the gods (*deva-yāniyo maggo*) appears before him. He visits heaven after heaven, starting at the lowest, and puts his question to the gods in each. They all say they don't know and ask him to try at the next level up. At the highest of the six god-worlds he is referred up to the 'Brahma-bodied gods' (*brahma-kāyikā devā*), so he now concentrates till he sees the path leading to Brahmā (*brahma-yāniyo maggo*). The Brahma-bodied gods in turn refer him up to Mahā Brahmā, who suddenly appears out of a flash of light. When the monk puts the question to him, Brahmā produces a rodomontade about how great he is – but ducks the question. The monk says he is not asking him how great he is but about where the four elements are destroyed. Finally (p. 221) Brahmā takes him by the arm, leads him aside, and tells him that the Brahma-bodied gods think he knows everything, and he doesn't like to disabuse them, so he couldn't admit it in front of them, but he too doesn't know the answer. He tells the monk he is a fool: the person whom he should have asked this question was the Buddha. So the monk duly 'disappeared in the Brahma-world and appeared before me'. How the Buddha solved the riddle I have already revealed.

It is obvious that this is satire, and that it is an allegory showing the Buddha's superiority to Brahmā (let alone lesser gods). But unless the gods with whom the monk converses have some kind of existence outside his own mind, and unless he has the power through meditation to travel to higher realms and back, the story simply doesn't work.

The subject with which the *Kevaddha Sutta* begins is the use of *iddhi*, supernormal powers. These powers include levitation and flying, walking on water and passing through solids. In this text the Buddha says that he finds the display of such powers loathsome and disgusting, because they can be achieved by magic, and so would not convert anyone (pp. 213-14). It is not that the Buddha does not believe in the possibility of such powers: on the contrary, he thinks they come too cheap. Moreover, as we have already remarked, the texts are not consistent about the Buddha's attitudes to such miracles; much seems to depend on the oircumstances. For example, in one text, the *Brahma-nimantaṇika Sutta* (MN *sutta* 49) he goes to the heaven of a Brahmā called Baka[20] and has the usual kind of debate with him, but caps it with a disappearing contest which he wins: Baka tries to disappear from his sight but cannot, whereupon the Buddha disappears from the sight of Baka and his retinue (MN I, 330). While invisible he recites a verse to them saying that he has not clung to becoming (*bhava*). Again, the exercise of *iddhi* appears to be an allegory here, expressing the Buddha's total

[20] Baka means 'heron'. Why should a Brahmā be called 'Heron'? Yet again, presumably this is a joke. In the Upaniṣads, Brahmā is called *haṃsa*, a wild goose. (In English this is often translated as 'swan' because 'goose' sounds undignified.) The heron is another large aquatic bird. In Indian fable it is associated with hypocrisy (see e.g. *The Panchatantra* trans. Franklin Edgerton (London, 1965), pp. 43-4).

understanding of life processes, but the fit is not very good. Moreover, there are far too many texts in which the Buddha and other monks exercise such powers for them all to be dismissed as nothing but conscious metaphor.

To those brought up in or close to the Christian tradition, the idea that a holy person may be able to perform miracles, in the sense of feats which go against the normal laws of nature, is quite familiar. But in the early Buddhist texts we find a blurring of boundaries which goes beyond such thaumaturgy. In the *Mahā Parinibbāna Sutta* the Buddha describes the causes of earthquakes (DN II, 107-8). The first he lists is that the earth rests on water and the water on wind, and when the wind blows hard the earth shakes. The second cause goes: 'A renunciate or brahmin has supernormal powers and has acquired control over his mind, or a deity of great power and influence (has done so); if he has developed a limited perception of earth and a boundless perception of water, he shakes the earth and makes it tremble.'

The second cause presupposes the cosmology of the first: that the earth rests on water. This view, reminiscent of pre-Socratic philosophy, is quite different from ancient India's religious cosmologies, including the Buddhist one, which are hierarchised from top to bottom. Later Buddhist systematisers had to tuck in the hells between the earth on which we stand and the water underneath (Gombrich, 1975:136).

The renunciate, brahmin or deity (not necessarily a Buddhist) has cultivated a certain perception (*saññā*) of earth and water. *Saññā*, the third of the five *khandha*, would best be translated 'apperception', were that term widely understood. *Saññā* carries a connotation of naming, so it refers to perceptions to which one can put a name, as distinct from mere consciousness of something being there (which is *viññāṇa*, the fifth *khandha*). In this case the meditator thinks of (we would say 'imagines') the earth as small and the waters beneath it as infinitely vast. The result, that the earth is tossed on the waters, is however publicly perceptible, so our 'imagines' does not fit. The very language of the text seems not to fit our suppositions about thought and perception, for the words are not that 'he has a perception of earth as limited and water as boundless'; the adjectives go with the perception, as if a perception were the size of its object. In this case, the perception even seems to determine the size of its object.

The same power of affecting the physical world by thought alone is illustrated in a canonical text from another early Buddhist tradition, the *Vinaya* of the Mahāsāṅghikas, which is preserved only in Chinese. This tradition is strict in prohibiting monks' touching women. One passage[21] considers what a monk is to do if he sees a woman drowning. If they are shipwrecked and she is floating towards him, he is allowed to help her out by means of a perception of earth. Presumably this means that he thinks of earth – which in Buddhism represents solidity in general – so that they both find something firm to stand on or hold on to. If he is walking along a river bank and a woman falls in and calls to him for help, he may get her out by perceiving earth, or by means of a rope or bamboo or piece of wood. Again, the perception of earth presumably means that he uses his mental powers to give the woman physical support.[22]

Earthquakes and saving lives are important topics. But the problem I have raised is more general. In SN IV, 93-7 = *sutta* XXXV, 116, the Buddha tells monks that it is not by going (i.e., by physical movement) that one can know, see and reach[23] the end of the world (*loka*); but without reaching the end of the world one cannot put an end to suffering. The monks ask Ānanda to explain, and he does so (with the Buddha's subsequent approval): 'In the discipline of the noble one, that is called "world" (*loka*) by

[21] *Taisho* 22.267b.2-10. I am indebted to the Ven. Juo-Hsüeh Shih for this information.

[22] The text goes on to say that if he (presumably for lack of these means) says, 'I know that you are in misery, but you should flow with your karma,' he has not committed an offence. If the woman grasps him, he must keep a watch on himself. Such texts allow one to understand how the Mahāyāna could accuse monks of being selfish.

[23] The language at this point is unusual: three future passive participles in *-ayya*. Geiger and Norman (*Pali Grammar* para 203) considers these very old forms. Are they traces of the Buddha's own pronunciation?

which in the world one comes to perceive the world (*loka-saññī hoti*) and be *loka-mānī* [see below]. By what is that? By the eye, the ear, the sense of smell, the tongue, the body and the mind (*manena*)' (p. 95 para.11).

I find this passage tantalisingly ambiguous. We have just seen that *saññā*, apperception, does not necessarily carry the implication we take for granted: that a subject perceives an independently existing object without thereby affecting that object. Usually the word will indeed mean that a perceiver recognises an object of perception. That is a process, and it is processes, I have argued, that concerned the Buddha. About the ontological status of subject and object, perceiver and perceived, he did not express a view. Thus the term *loka-saññī* does not tell us whether there really is a world 'out there' or not.

The word *loka-mānī* I have left untranslated. It would accord with general Pali style for the two words *loka-saññī* and *loka-mānī* to be near synonyms, but such apparent parallelism can also be misleading, as we shall see in the next chapter. The commentary (*Sārattha-ppakāsinī* II,389) assumes near synonymity. It correctly derives *mānī* from the verbal root *man* 'to think', and takes *loka-mānī* to mean 'thinking of/about the world'. The problem with this is that *mānin* at the end of a compound (the word and usage are common to Sanskrit and Pali) never seems to mean simply 'thinking of'. It seems always to have a reflexive sense, 'thinking oneself to be *x*', as in *paṇḍita-mānin*, 'thinking oneself to be very clever'. (From this it slips into meaning 'proud of being *x*'.) So what does *loka-mānī* mean? By strict analogy with the common usage it should mean 'thinking oneself to be the world'.

Is this what Ānanda and the Buddha meant? It would not convey a solipsistic ontology, as they did not aim to convey any ontology at all. It might well, however, convey a moral message; that people think the world of themselves, thinking that they are the world; they emotionally equate the world with their experience of it.

What Ānanda goes on to say is that the world (in the only sense that matters) is our experiences through the six senses (the five plus the mind), so that what the Buddha meant is that salvation can come only by putting an end to those experiences.

I see another possible interpretation of *loka-mānī*. Words like *paṇḍita-mānī* carry the implication that when one thinks oneself *x* one is wrong. So perhaps here *mānī* does not have its usual reflexive meaning but carries the implication of falsity: 'thinking that there is a world'.

What this adds up to, if I am correct, is that the text leaves itself open to either interpretation: an idealist ontology like that later espoused by the Buddhist school of *vijñāna-vāda*, or a realist ontology like that of the Theravāda. The Buddha, probably deliberately, took neither view. But at the same time his very presuppositions about the relations between what goes on in our heads and what is 'out there' may have been unlike ours. If that is so, it would make such questions as 'Does a Buddha exist after death?'[24] truly unanswerable.

[24] This is one of a set of questions which the Buddha said he did not intend to answer (MN *sutta* 63).

IV

Retracing an Ancient Debate: How Insight Worsted Concentration in the Pali Canon

This chapter is concerned with a set of instances of historical change and doctrinal development within the Pali Canon. The most important of these changes is the development of the idea that Enlightenment can be attained without meditation, by a process of intellectual analysis (technically known as *paññā*, insight) alone. This idea is perhaps made fully explicit in only two texts of the *Sutta Piṭaka*; but even one would be enough to authorise practice. There has certainly survived in Theravāda Buddhism a tradition of behaviour which takes these texts as its authority. There is also a Buddhist Sanskrit text (but preserved only in Chinese translation), Harivarman's *Satya-siddhi-śāstra*[1] which uses the same canonical material to reach the same conclusion; but this work belongs to an extinct school of the Śrāvakayāna (the Bahuśrutīya).[2] So far as I know, the Theravāda is the only surviving form of Buddhism to accept this idea.

This chapter posits two particular processes of change, both referred to in my opening lecture. One is scholastic literalism, a form of exegesis which reads into words and phrases more meaning than was originally intended, in order to create distinctions. The other is debate. The Buddhist Canon was compiled by a number of monks, and internal evidence makes it clear that not every text that has come down to us in the *Sutta Piṭaka* can have been recited by Ānanda at the First Communal Recitation. The texts contain many and sometimes discrepant

[1] Reconstructed Sanskrit text and English translation by N.Aiyaswami Sastri, Oriental Institute, Baroda, vol.1 1975, vol.2 1978. Modern scholars date it to the third century A.D.

[2] Strictly speaking, Harivarman accepts a tiny bit of concentration (*samādhi*), but only below the level of the first *jhāna* (de La Vallée Poussin, 1936-7:201-2).

accounts of such central topics as meditation. As I have written elsewhere, one likely reason for the discrepancies is that in the course of a preaching career lasting forty-five years the Buddha formulated things in various ways and perhaps even changed his mind (Gombrich, 1990:9). But another reason I posit for discrepancies is that monks were arguing about these topics and that the texts sometimes preserve more than one side of an argument. These two processes are not mutually exclusive: scholastic literalism can provide ample matter for debate, and argument can often degenerate into nit-picking![3]

* * *

In the *Puggala-paññatti*, which T.W. Rhys Davids considered to be the earliest of the books in the *Abhidhamma Piṭaka* (Rhys Davids 1903:188), people are classified by moral and spiritual types. The work is not original: the classifications are drawn from the *Sutta Piṭaka*. The text contains[4] a seven-fold classification:

ubhato-bhāga-vimutto	released on both sides
paññā-vimutto	released by insight
kāya-sakkhī	bodily witness
diṭṭhi-ppatto	who has seen the point
saddhā-vimutto	released by faith
dhammânusārī	follower of the teaching
saddhânusārī	follower through faith

[3] To preclude a misunderstanding voiced at the seminar, let me emphasise that I do not think that disagreement and doctrinal change arose only from over-literal exegesis of texts. I have never denied that many of the debates, including the one which this chapter analyses, were about real issues.

[4] *Puggala-paññatti* 10 and 72.

This seven-fold classification[5] is also contained within a nine-fold classification in which the first two items are:

sammā-sambuddho	fully Enlightened
pacceka-sambuddho	Enlightened individually

This makes it immediately obvious that we are dealing with a hierarchy, in which the 'follower through faith' ranks last.

This list of nine is further extended to a list of ten in the *Sutta Piṭaka*, at AN V, 23. This text lists the ten types worthy of offerings, etc. – the standard description of the Sangha. After the 'follower through faith' it adds *gotrabhū*,[6] 'family member'.

Similarly, the list of seven is found in the *Sutta Piṭaka* contained within a list of nine which is extended in another way. At AN I, 73-4 the Buddha warns monks not to gossip in front of the laity, categorising each other. The categories he envisages their using are the seven, plus

sīlavā kalyāṇa-dhammo	virtuous and good
dussīlo pāpa-dhammo	immoral and wicked

AN IV, 215 has the same list of nine, in a similar context.

However, the list of seven most frequently occurs in the *Sutta Piṭaka* by itself, without extensions, and it constitutes our real starting point. It occurs several times as a bald list, with no explanation of the terms: at DN III, 105; DN III, 253-4; MN I, 439; AN IV, 10. Similarly, the terms are listed without explanation within the longer lists cited above from AN I, 73-4, AN IV, 215 and AN V, 23.

[5] *Puggala-paññatti* 10, 14-15, 73-4. The terms are also listed on p. 3.

[6] It would not be relevant here to discuss this problematic technical term, which has long been recognised (see P.E.D. *s.v.*) as alien to the earliest texts. For discussion see Ruegg, 1974; von Hinüber, 1978; Takasaki, 1992.

The only text in the *Sutta Piṭaka* in which the list is described in a way which differentiates between the terms is the *Kīṭāgiri Sutta*, MN *sutta* 70. There is also a *sutta*, AN IV, 74-9, in which the first six of the terms in our list are described, but in a way that merely divides them into two categories; this text I shall deal with after I have recorded all that the texts have to tell us about the seven terms while they appear as a list. For this record I shall also introduce the information available from the *Puggala-paññatti*.

The context in which the list occurs in the *Kīṭāgiri Sutta* is as follows.

The Buddha asks monks not to eat in the evening (literally: at night), but certain monks are reluctant to stop doing so. Thereupon he says that not everyone needs to be so careful: *arahant*s need not be careful because they are incapable of going wrong. But those still in training (*sekhā*) must be careful (MN I, 477). Then, to illustrate who needs to take care (and avoid an evening meal) he lists our seven types, explaining each and saying whether each needs to take care – i.e., whether he is already an *arahant*.

The explanations are given in terms of the *vimokkha*, eight graded meditative states (see P.E.D. *s.v.*) which culminate in the extinction of apperception and feeling, and the *āsava*, a set of three or four defects, extinction of which is tantamount to attaining nirvana: sensual desire, desire for continued existence, speculative views (sometimes omitted), ignorance. I shall translate *vimo(k)khā* 'releases' and *āsavā* 'corruptions'.

1. The one 'released on both sides' is described thus: 'A certain type touches with his body and stays in these tranquil releases which are formless, transcending forms, and his corruptions are destroyed by seeing with his insight.' *ekacco puggalo ye te santā vimokhā atikkamma rūpe āruppā te kāyena phassitvā viharati, paññāya c'assa disvā āsavā parikkhīṇā honti* (p. 477).

2. The one 'released by insight' 'does not touch with his body and stay in ...' – the rest is identical. The Pali is identical except that there is the word *na* between *te* and *kāyena*.
3. The 'bodily witness' 'touches with his body and stays in those tranquil releases ... transcending forms, and some of his corruptions are destroyed ....' The Pali is the same as for the first except that there is the word *ekacce* before *āsavā*.
4. The one 'who has seen the point' 'does not touch with his body ... some of his corruptions are destroyed ... With his insight he has understood and penetrated the things taught by the Tathāgata.' The Pali has the *na* as under 2 and the *ekacce* as under 3; then comes *Tathāgatappaveditā c'assa dhammā vodiṭṭhā honti vocaritā*.
5. The one 'released by faith' 'does not touch with his body ... some of his corruptions are destroyed .... His faith in the Tathāgata is settled and firmly rooted.' The first part is as under 4; then comes *Tathāgate c'assa saddhā niviṭṭhā hoti mūlajātā patiṭṭhitā*.
6. The 'follower of the teaching' 'does not touch with his body ... transcending forms, and his corruptions are not destroyed by seeing with his insight. Through his insight he finds a measure of satisfaction in the things taught by the Tathāgata, and he has the faculties of faith, energy, awareness, concentration and insight.' The Pali has the *na* as under 2, then reads *āsavā aparikkhīṇā*; then comes *Tathāgatappaveditā c' assa dhammā paññāya mattaso nijjhānaṃ khamanti, api c'assa ime dhammā honti seyyathīdaṃ saddhindriyaṃ viriyindriyaṃ satindriyaṃ samādhindriyaṃ paññindriyaṃ*.
7. The 'follower through faith' 'does not touch with his body ... transcending forms, and his corruptions are not destroyed ... insight. He only has faith in and affection for the Tathāgata, and he has the faculties ... insight'. The first part is as under 6; then comes *Tathāgate c'assa saddhāmattaṃ hoti pemamattaṃ, api c'assa ime* ... (as under 6).

All this is summarised diagramatically in Figure 1.

	touches releases with the body	corruptions destroyed by insight	faith	*arahant*
1. released on both sides	yes	yes	n/a	yes
2. released by insight	no	yes	n/a	yes
3. bodily witness	yes	some	n/a	no
4. who has seen the point	no	some	n/a	no
5. released by faith	no	some	yes	no
6. follower of the teaching	no	no	some *	no
7. follower through faith	no	no	yes	no

*6 also has some concentration and insight, but he is predominantly an insight type (*sic*).

Figure 1. The Seven Types.

Of each type from 3 to 7 inclusive the text says that under favourable conditions (which are described in a long sentence) he may attain Enlightenment in this life.

It is convenient at this point to add the supplementary information provided by *Puggala-paññatti* p. 15. The descriptions of the first three types are the same as in the *Kīṭāgiri*

Sutta, somewhat abbreviated. The other four descriptions have a little more detail:

4. The one 'who has seen the point' has insight into the four noble truths. 'With his insight ...' (as above); then 'by his insight some of his corruptions are destroyed'.

5. The 'released by faith' is exactly the same as the previous one, with the addition at the end of the words 'but not as for him who has seen the point' (*no ca kho yathā diṭṭhipattassa*).

6. 'When the faculty of insight of the type who is on the way to realising the result of stream-entry[7] is very great, and brings insight[8], he develops the noble path which is introduced by insight. He is called the type "follower of the teaching". When one is on the way to realising the result of stream-entry, one is the type "follower of the teaching"; when one has that result one is one who has seen the point.'

7. 'When the faculty of faith of the type who is on the way to realising the result of stream-entry is very great, and brings faith,[9] he develops the noble path which is introduced by faith. He is called the type "follower through faith". When one is on the way to realising the result of stream-entry, one is the type "follower through faith"; when one has that result one is "released by faith".'

[7] Those whose progress towards Enlightenment is irreversible are classified in four grades; in ascending order: stream-enterer, once-returner, non-returner, ***arahant*** (=Enlightened). The stream-enterer has at most seven more lives, the once-returner at most one (as a human being), the non-returner no more as a human being (only in a high heaven), and an *arahant*, being already Enlightened, cannot be reborn.

[8] Reading *paññāvāhī* with MA II, 120, which quotes this passage.

[9] Reading *saddhāvāhī* with MA II, 120 (see previous note).

This goes a step further in systematisation than the *Kīṭāgiri Sutta*, in that it explicitly states that 4 and 5 are higher grades of 6 and 7 respectively. The paragraph on 7 makes it obvious that the text of the paragraph on 5 is corrupt. A copyist accidentally repeated for 5 the paragraph applying to 4. Then he, or a later scribe, noticing the identity of the two descriptions, feebly added the last clause. One could emend the text with some confidence by resorting to the *Kīṭāgiri Sutta*.

Our list as thus expounded has an extremely schematic character, evidence of an attempt to systematise a variety of things which have been said in other texts about stages of spiritual progress. Nevertheless it contains two *prima facie* oddities. Firstly: the fifth type in the list is called 'released by faith', and yet he is not released at all; in fact he is placed third down the list of the unreleased. In the case of this type there is a straightforward contradiction between his title and its explanation. Secondly: it is an oddity, though not quite a contradiction, that in the list of seven there are just two who are released, and what determines whether one is released is whether one's 'corruptions are destroyed by seeing with insight'. There is an attainment, common to only the first and third on the list, which consists in reaching certain 'formless' meditative states, which are even called 'releases'; but they do not release! Thus the attainment of those 'releases' by the first and highest type, the 'one released both ways', seems to have no function, but to hang there as a redundant ornament, like an act of supererogation in Roman Catholicism.

* * *

Before we set out to explore these anomalies, let us look at AN IV, 74-9, the only other text which has anything to say about this list, even though it is not particularly helpful. Here the list occurs during a dialogue which takes place in a heaven. A monk called Tissa has recently been reborn as a Brahmā, and Moggallāna calls on him to ask him about the knowledge gods may have of human spiritual attainments. Tissa speaks of the first six in our list. Of each of the first two types he says that as long as his body exists gods and men will see him, but after the dissolution of the body they will not. Of each of the next four he says that under favourable conditions they may attain Enlightenment; this sentence is identical to the one used five times, for types 3 to 7, in the *Kīṭāgiri Sutta*.

Moggallāna returns to the Buddha and tells him of his talk with the late Tissa. The Buddha then makes up the list to seven, but in an unusual way. He says, 'Tissa didn't teach you about the type who stays in the signless (*animitta-vihāriṃ*).' At Moggallāna's request, he explains that 'by not attending to any signs a monk enters and stays in signless mental concentration', and the gods know of him too that under favourable conditions – detailed as for the previous four types – he may attain Enlightenment.

How are we to interpret this text? It seems to me to be part of a debate among the authors/compilers/reciters of our texts. This debate concerns the relative value of various moral qualities and spiritual attainments, value being measured by how close they bring you to Enlightenment. The compiler of this little text has received our list of seven types. In this list three qualities are evidently jockeying for position. They are three of the five faculties (*indriya*): faith, concentration and insight. Insight is winning easily: it is the only one of the three to bring release (types 1 and 2), and it also predominates in types 4 and 6. Faith has places 5 and 7. Concentration is up along with insight in first position, but there, as we have seen, it seems to play no role. Otherwise concentration predominates only at number 3, where it is present in full measure – but still not all that effective. Moreover, a type with a small amount of insight gets onto the list (at 6), but a small amount of concentration counts for nothing here.

The author of AN IV, 74-9 is, I think, trying to remedy that situation. The 'signless mental concentration' is synonymous with the 'formless releases', or approximately so. The author evidently feels that he cannot make an attack on the position of insight in the hierarchy: it is entrenched. Faith, however, is a far weaker opponent: someone 'released by faith' is in fact not released at all! So in this debate between proponents of the three qualities, the 'follower through faith' loses his position in the table of types who have reached or are headed for Enlightenment to a proponent of concentration.

* * *

There is direct evidence in the texts for the kind of debate I have here posited. A straightforward example is to be found at AN I, 118-120. Three monks – Saviṭṭha, Mahākoṭṭhita and Sāriputta – are discussing which of the following three types is best: the bodily witness, the one who has seen the point, or the one released by faith (numbers 3, 4 and 5 in our list). Saviṭṭha chooses the one released by faith, 'because his faculty of faith is outstanding' (*imassa puggalassa saddhindriyaṃ adhimattaṃ*). (As often, what is presented as a reason is merely a tautologous rephrasing.) In the same terms, Mahākoṭṭhita prefers the bodily witness because his faculty of concentration is outstanding, and Sāriputta the one who has seen the point because of his faculty of insight. They consult the Buddha. He replies that one cannot easily decide definitively (*ekaṃsena*) which type is best, for any of the three may become a once-returner, a non-returner or an *arahant*. In other words, anyone who can be described as any of these three types has made considerable spiritual progress, having at most one more life to live through after this one; and any of these three faculties may also take one all the way to Enlightenment.

I need hardly repeat that no text in the Canon can be a perfect record, in the literal modern sense, of what the Buddha (and his interlocutors) said: the texts were composed by their original reciters and bear obvious traces of the formalisation and standardisation typical of oral literature. The *sutta* I have just discussed is very formalised indeed, even to the extent that the faculties of faith, concentration and insight are presented in what was settled as the correct order. The five faculties (faith, energy, awareness, concentration and insight) are one of those numbered lists which serve as mnemonics for the essentials of the doctrine, and may well go back to the Buddha's own lifetime. The sequence in these lists need not necessarily indicate ranking, but that implication was often drawn.

Despite its extremely standardised formulation, the text seems to me to represent just the kind of incident that must often have happened to the Buddha, as it does to any religious teacher. Disciples argue about the best way to attain salvation, each stressing what seems to him to be his own strong point, and then they put their doubts before the teacher; he in turn gives them a reassuring (and doubtless wise) answer: there are various paths to the one goal.

Let us now compare the contents of this text to our list of seven types (which, it will be seen, I do *not* ascribe to the Buddha's lifetime). Here the term 'released by faith' does make sense, because the type designated can actually achieve Enlightenment. But so can the two who precede him in the list. Here the 'bodily witness' and he 'who has seen the point' are not necessarily as yet falling short of the ultimate attainment. In contrast to that list, those three types may all be *arahant*s. In sum, we may draw two conclusions from the comparison. First: that here Enlightenment may be won by either faith or concentration or insight, whereas in the list of seven it is won only by insight. This must be of interest for the early history of Buddhism. Second: that the type who is here designated 'he who sees the point' is the same, at least at the top level of his attainment, as the one 'released by insight' in the list of seven. This is a narrower point, but interesting as an indicator showing that the list of seven must be a purely scholastic construction: scholastic in the sense that it makes distinctions which are verbal only and do not refer to any distinctions in reality.

I think that it can be shown that almost every feature of the list of seven types can be traced back to scholasticism in this sense: a dependence upon words, at the cost of disregarding what those words were originally intended to describe.

* * *

To exemplify this process, let us examine the bottom of our list and look at the history of the types 'follower of the teaching' and 'follower through faith'.

At the end of the *Alagaddūpama Sutta* (MN *sutta* 22), a text which I consider to have several features which suggest that it is among the oldest, the Buddha says that he has taught quite plainly and openly, and that monks who follow his teachings to a greater or lesser extent will correspondingly make greater or lesser spiritual progress. In the repetitious oral style, the text each time repeats the phrases about clear teaching and then describes the progress of a category of follower, starting with the best, the *arahant*s. There are altogether six such paragraphs with identical beginnings about the clear teaching, so one can deduce that there are six graded ranks of followers. In second place, after the *arahant*s, come the non-returners; third the once-returners; fourth the stream-enterers. This is absolutely standard, and so are the descriptions of those grades. Sixth and last come 'those who only have faith in me and affection for me: they are all bound for heaven' *(yesaṃ mayi saddhā-mattaṃ pema-mattaṃ sabbe te sagga-parāyaṇā*.).

In the fifth, penultimate position are those who interest us at the moment. The text is very brief: *ye te bhikkhū dhammânusārino saddhânusārino sabbe te sambodhi-parāyanā*. I translate: 'The monks who follow my teaching, following through faith: they are all bound for Enlightenment.' From the structure of the passage it seems to me absolutely clear that we are here dealing with a single category.

The commentary, of course, does not agree, because it follows the scholastic classifications such as our list of seven; in fact it quotes the *Puggala-paññatti* (p. 15) to the effect that the 'follower of the teaching' is a type strong in the faculty of insight but a grade down from the 'one who has seen the point', whereas the 'follower through faith' is the type strong in the faculty of faith but a grade down from the one 'released by faith'. But the commentary is not sensitive to the structure of the text.

My main point is that the *dhammânusārino* and the *saddhânusārino* are here – originally – the same people. My interpretation differs from the one which became traditional in other ways as well. I think that it is clear from the context that *dhammânusārin* simply means 'following the teaching' and has nothing to do with *dhammā* (plural) in a technical sense (such as 'phenomena') or with the particular cultivation of one faculty rather than another. I think that in this text the two compounds *dhammânusārino saddhânusārino* are not quite on the same footing; one could even regard the latter word as qualifying the former. In no interpretation, in fact, are the two compounds perfectly parallel grammatically, since *dhamma* must be the direct object of 'following' whereas *saddhā* has to be interpreted as an instrumental or an ablative – 'with faith' or 'through faith'

In the *Cūḷa Gopālaka Sutta* (MN *sutta* 34) the categories are virtually the same as in the *Alagaddūpama Sutta*. The text consists of an extended simile, in which monks are compared to cattle crossing the Ganges. Here there are only five categories and the *dhammânusārino saddhânusārino* constitute the last of them; but again the structure of the text makes it absolutely clear that those two words refer to a single category: they are like the new-born calf who is carried across the river by following his mother's lowing.

The differentiation between *dhammânusārī* and *saddhânusārī* must have occurred when the four grades of spiritual progress, *arahant* down to stream-enterer, were listed, and the words *dhammânusārino saddhânusārino* appended, in isolation, not within a wider context. Under those circumstances it could be natural to deduce that *saddhânusārino* was a category separate from *dhammânusārino* and ranked lower. I cannot prove exactly where or when this deduction occurred, but SN V, 200 gives an idea of what I mean. Here there is a short text (*sutta* 12) in the section on the five faculties (*Indriya-saṃyutta*). In the previous short text (*sutta* 11) the five faculties are explained hierarchically, with faith at the bottom and insight ranking top. *Sutta* 12 says that the *arahant* has developed the five faculties completely, the non-returner more moderately (*mudutara*), the once-returner yet more moderately, the stream-enterer ditto, the *dhammânusārī* ditto, the *saddhânusārī* ditto. So here the *saddhânusārī* ranks below the *dhammânusārī*.

The only text I know of which gives a little more substance to this differential – until we reach our list of seven – is SN III, 225, which in the paragraphs that interest us is identical with SN III, 227-8. At III, 225 all of the six organs of the senses are said to be impermanent and liable to change; at III, 227 the same is said of the five aggregates (*khandha*). Both texts continue:

O monks, one who has faith in and feels sure about these teachings (*dhammā*) is called a follower through faith; he has entered on the way to correctness; he has entered the stage of good men (*sappurisa-bhūmi*) and passed beyond the stage of ordinary unenlightened people (*puthujjana-bhūmi*). He cannot do anything which would cause him to be reborn in hell or as an animal or ghost. He cannot die until he has experienced for himself the result of stream-entry.

O monks, one who through his insight finds a measure of satisfaction in these teachings is called a follower of the teaching; he has entered ....' (The rest of the paragraph is identical to the previous paragraph.)

O monks, one who knows and sees things like this is called a stream-enterer, not liable to relapse, assured, bound for Enlightenment.

Here the *dhammânusārī* is differentiated from the *saddhânusārī*, but in such nuanced terms that if this text were taken in isolation the only thing that would make one sure that he is ranked higher is that the next type mentioned is the stream-enterer. The phrase which is peculiar to the *dhammânusārī* is the same as that used in the *Kīṭāgiri Sutta* to define him. Which text is the originator and which the borrower one cannot say.

When we look back at the definitions of these two types in the *Kīṭāgiri Sutta*, we notice that the *saddhânusārī* is positively defined mainly by the fact that he 'only has faith in and affection for the Tathāgata'. The phrase is apparently borrowed from the sixth and final category in the *Alagaddūpama Sutta.* The need felt to differentiate the *dhammânusārī* from the *saddhânusārī* has led to a slight distortion of that passage, a distortion which adds plausibility to our tracing of the line of development.

I believe that this discussion covers all informative occurrences of the terms *dhammânusārī* and *saddhânusārī*. For their mention in the list of seven or its extensions, the references have been given above.

* * *

Now that we have seen how debate and scholastic literalism combined to form the lower half of our original list, we turn our attention to the top three types in the list. We recall that despite the Buddha's statement in AN I, 118-120, the compiler of this list will not allow that faith or concentration can be the faculties with which to gain nirvana; for him the only faculty which can do that is insight.

The competition between meditation and insight as the effective method by which to achieve nirvana is the topic of a justly famous article by Louis de La Vallée Poussin: 'Musīla et Nārada: Le Chemin de Nirvāṇa' (de La Vallée Poussin, 1936-7). Though I do not entirely agree with what he says – to begin with, I do not think that either 'ascetic' or 'ecstatic' is an appropriate description of Buddhist meditation – I have thought it useful here to give a translation of the beginning of his article (minus its first paragraph), and do so in the Appendix.

I see the devaluation of concentration as originating in certain identifiable texts. One of them is called the *Susīma Sutta* (SN II, 119-128). This is the text, de La Vallée Poussin tells us (p. 201), on which Harivarman based his position that one could attain release without entering any of the *jhāna*, the stages of concentration. As the text stands in Pali – and apparently as Harivarman read it – it does indeed appear to support that position. However, by comparing it with its Chinese version and by scrutinising its internal coherence, I think I have established that the extant Pali *Susīma Sutta* is a reworking of an older text – one might almost describe it as a kind of forgery. To do justice to the *Susīma Sutta* requires so much space that I intend to devote a separate article to it. Here I shall merely extract the conclusions essential to my more general argument.

Before I do that, however, I must trace the route by which *paññā-vimutto*, 'released by insight', came to be seen as half of the obscure concept 'released on both sides'. Our investigation of this begins with the corresponding abstract noun, *paññā-vimutti*.

How should we translate *paññā*? The P.E.D. entry begins: 'intelligence, comprising all the higher faculties of cognition, "intellect as conversant with general truths" (Dial. II, 68), reason, wisdom, insight, knowledge, recognition.' Paul Williams has written a fine account of the Sanskrit equivalent, *prajñā*, in the context of the early Mahāyāna (Williams, 1990). I quote his first sentences:

> Wisdom is, alas, all too rare; *prajñā* is not. This apparent paradox should make us sensitive to the usual translation of '*prajñā*' by 'wisdom'. *Prajñā* is a mental event, a state of consciousness, normally in the Indo-Tibetan context a state of consciousness which results from analysis, investigation.' (p. 42)

Williams then shows how by successive shifts of meaning *prajñā* comes to mean '*correct* discernment of the true situation' (p. 43, my italics), thence 'a meditative absorption the content of which is the ultimate truth' (ibid), which (in early Mahāyāna) 'is non-conceptual and non-dual, whereas the preceding examples have been conceptual' (p. 44), and finally 'the content or object of such an ultimate awareness' (ibid). The two latter meanings are not applicable to *paññā* in our texts, but the two former ones are: they tend to use *paññā* to denote *correct* understanding. At bottom, however, *paññā* is simply a verbal noun denoting 'a mental event', as Williams well puts it. In English the word 'insight' generally carries the implication that the insight is correct, so I think it is a good translation for *paññā*, provided that one remembers not to reify the concept. So I translate *paññā-vimutti* as 'release by insight'.

When the word *paññā-vimutti* appears in the texts it is usually paired with *ceto-vimutti*. The P.E.D. says of *ceto* that it equals *citta*, and on the latter it has an enormous article. As it says, 'in Indian Psychology *citta* is the seat and organ of thought'; it also simply means 'thought' or 'thinking'. Since the general tenor of the Buddha's teaching, with its emphasis on impermanence and lack of essence, was to substitute process for substance, English 'thought', with its dynamic connotations, will in many contexts be preferable to the more static 'mind'. However, since the texts also use the expression *cittaṃ vimuccati*, and one can hardly say in English that 'thought is freed', I shall here translate *ceto-vimutti* as 'release of the mind'. Note that this means that, just as with the words *dhammânusārino saddhânusārino*, we have here a pair of compounds, a doublet, in which the syntactical relationship of the first half to the second half varies: 'release *of* the mind' but 'release *by* insight'.

Just as was the case with *dhammânusārino* and *saddhânusārino*, I do not think that these words originated as technical terms. I suppose there is probably no psychological term in the early Buddhist texts which did not finally come to be classified by the *abhidhamma* and so acquire a technical meaning; and certainly *citta/ceto* and *paññā* have precise meanings in systematised dogmatics. Originally, however, *citta/ceto* is not one of the five aggregates (*khandha*), but a general term for mind or thought, just as *paññā* begins as a general term for understanding.

Because the compounds *ceto-vimutti* and *paññā-vimutti* differ in syntax, they do not have quite the same meaning; but they originally have the same reference. (Again: we recall that *dhammânusārī* and *saddhânusārī*, though different in meaning, also originally had the same reference.) There is only one release: it is a mental event, triggered by insight. The practical problem is how to reach that stage.

However, for the Buddhist tradition my assumptions that these are not technical terms but that they are near-synonyms with the same reference are problematic. At MN I, 437, Ānanda asks the Buddha why some monks are *ceto-vimuttino* and some *paññā-vimuttino*. The Buddha does not reply, as in effect he did to the three monks at AN I, 118-120, that there is no answer to this question. On the contrary, he says, with extreme brevity, that it is due to disparity in their faculties (*ettha kho tesâhaṃ Ānanda indriya-vemattataṃ vadāmi*). This text thus strongly suggests that there are two *vimutti*, two qualitatively different experiences of release. I hope to show below that this text is the product of a scholastic debate.

The tradition came to see the two terms as a contrasting pair. There are several *suttas* with which we could illustrate this contrast. Let us look as AN I, 61:

O monks, there are these two things conducive to gnosis. Which? Calm and intuition.[10] What advantage does one enjoy by developing calm? The mind is developed. What advantage does one enjoy by developing one's mind? Passion is abandoned. What advantage does one enjoy by developing intuition? Insight is developed. What advantage does one enjoy by developing insight? Ignorance is abandoned. Monks, the mind defiled by passion is not released; insight defiled by ignorance is not developed. Thus,[11] monks, through dispassion for passion there is release of the mind, through dispassion for ignorance[12] there is release by insight.

[10] To translate *vipassanā* I would have preferred 'insight', but I have already used that for *paññā*, so I have gone along with F. L. Woodward, the P.T.S. translator (Woodward, 1932:55). *Paññā* and *vipassanā* have the same basic meaning but as technical terms are used in different contexts.

[11] Reading *iti*.

[12] An awkward result of this artificial dichotomy lies in the strange compound *avijjā-virāga*, 'dispassion for ignorance'. *Virāga*, dispassion, is used as a synonym for nirvana in various standard formulae (see P.E.D. *s.v.*). The attainment of nirvana is the same as the abolition of passion, hatred and delusion. *Virāga* is a suitable term for the abolition of the first two; but now that a dichotomy has been introduced into that attainment, it is clumsily divided into *rāga-virāga*, a tautology, and *avijjā-virāga*, a nonsensical term.

The above passage, which we have translated *in toto*, seems (like many others) to suggest two paths to nirvana. That there are two such methods is an idea deeply embedded in the doctrine of the Buddha,[13] but our problem revolves around how this idea is to be interpreted. Few teachings seem to be more fundamental than that the noble eightfold path can be divided into the stages *sīla*, *samādhi*, *paññā*: morality, concentration, insight. All texts agree that morality is the prerequisite for spiritual progress. Then what is the relationship between what one may most appropriately call (to vary the translation for this context) meditation and understanding?

Four views can be found in the texts. First: the above three-fold formulation naturally lends itself to a ranked interpretation: that each stage is a prerequisite for the next; that meditation is a training essential for understanding. This has probably been the most widespread interpretation. It shades into a second possible interpretation: that to attain nirvana both methods must to some extent be employed, but that either may be given priority. (A Pali expression for this, *samatha-/vipassanā-pubbaṃgamaṃ ariya-maggaṃ bhāveti*, is quoted from the *Niddesa* below.) This is probably the interpretation reflected in AN I, 61 above: the statement, 'a mind defiled by passion is not released', precludes the possibility of reaching nirvana by developing insight, and so eliminating ignorance, alone.

For our current purposes the main importance of this second interpretation is that it is a bridge to a third interpretation: that the two methods are *alternatives*. Either may lead to Enlightenment, but maybe that Enlightenment is qualitatively different according to the method used. This is implied by Ānanda's question to the Buddha quoted above from MN I, 437. It is the interpretation set forth by de La Vallée Poussin at the beginning of his article (see Appendix), where he is trying to characterise ancient Buddhism

[13] This is because our predicament has a dual source: emotional (desire) and intellectual (ignorance). The two of course reinforce each other.

as a whole; he goes on, however, to cite texts supporting a fourth view.

This fourth view, the most extreme, may be a polemical response to the third one. It goes back to the original hierarchisation of meditation and understanding, but asserts that the latter is so superior to the former that it may be used alone, whereas meditation on its own can never achieve Enlightenment. We have seen this view represented in our list, or perhaps I should say in the passages of exegesis of the list quoted early in this paper. In other words, this interpretation says that if there are two *vimutti*, one of them is not really a *vimutti* at all. That it was possible to hold such a position, even though it created a paradox in the terminology, we have already shown above in the case of the 'released by faith'.

Even the first of these four interpretations lends itself to dichotomising between states and processes found in the one method or the other: on any of the latter three, such dichotomising becomes almost inevitable. By contrast, such early formulations of the path to Enlightenment as the four *jhāna* contain elements from both of what were later formulated as two sides: for example, the *jhāna* are themselves assigned to *samādhi*, but the third and fourth *jhāna* include *sati*, awareness. This may be clarified by a table (Figure 2) of some terms typically assigned to the two methods, once the dichotomy is in place.

to abolish passion (*rāga*)/ greed (*lobha*) and hatred (*dosa*)	to abolish ignorance (*avijjā*)/delusion (*moha*)
concentration (*samādhi*)	insight (*paññā*)
one-pointedness of mind (*cittass' ekaggatā*)	awareness (*sati*)
calming (*samatha*)	intuition (*vipassanā*)
jhāna etc. (enstatic states)	seeing reality (*yathā-bhūta-dassana*)
meditation (*bhāvanā*)	intellectual analysis (*paṭisambhidā*)
ceto-vimutti	*paññā-vimutti*

Figure 2. The Two Methods/Paths. (See also Appendix.)

* * *

It is a standard feature of the style of the *suttas* that words appear in pairs which are synonymous or nearly so. This feature is so pervasive that one need hardly argue for it: it occurs on every page. Sometimes the strings of synonyms or near-synonyms are longer: three or four are quite common. Sometimes the same technique is applied to whole phrases. We get synonymity of both words and phrases in such standard formulae as *saddhiṃ sammodi, sammodanīyaṃ kathaṃ sārāṇīyaṃ vītisāretvā* (e.g. at MN I, 16). This redundancy is a technique typical of oral literature to ensure transmission of the message.

On the other hand, it is equally typical of disciples and exegetes to pick over the words of the master to try to extract every grain of meaning from them. If he used two words to express something, say the exegetes, there must surely be a doctrinal rationale for that.

Here I hope to show that this is what happened to the doublet *ceto-vimutti paññā-vimutti*.

Let us analyse one of the commonest formulae for the attainment of nirvana. *Āsavānaṃ khayā anāsavaṃ ceto-vimuttiṃ paññā-vimuttiṃ diṭṭhe va dhamme sayaṃ abhiññā sacchikatvā upasampajja viharati*: 'through the waning away of the corruptions, himself in this very life[14] realises, witnesses, attains and stays in the corruption-free release of mind, release by insight.' One could argue at enormous length about exactly how much redundancy there is in this expression, but one could not deny that there is a lot: for example, that *anāsavaṃ* ('corruption-free') is redundant, and that the string of three absolutives (*abhiññā* etc.) could be reduced to two, or even to one, without

[14] I have translated *diṭṭhe va dhamme* in accordance with the tradition, but have a strong suspicion that the tradition is wrong and that it means 'when he has seen the truth'. This, however, must be matter for a later article.

affecting the meaning. Similarly, *ceto-vimutti* and *paññā-vimutti* cannot but refer to the same thing.

For corroboration let me quote the culmination of a passage which is famous as one of the longest and most explicit accounts in the *suttas* of the attainment of nirvana. In the *Sāmañña-phala Sutta* the final attainment of the fruit of the life of a renunciate is described as follows. One achieves true insight (*yathā-bhūtaṃ pajānāti*) into the four noble truths and their application to the corruptions; this is expressed in a series of eight parallel short sentences ending with *ayaṃ āsava-nirodha-gāminī paṭipadā ti yathā-bhūtaṃ pajānāti*: 'He has the true insight that this is the path leading to the destruction of the corruptions.' The text continues: *Tassa evaṃ jānato evaṃ passato kāmâsavā pi cittaṃ vimuccati bhavâsavā pi cittaṃ vimuccati avijjâsavā pi cittaṃ vimuccati. Vimuttasmiṃ vimuttam iti ñāṇaṃ hoti. Khīṇā jāti vusitaṃ brahma-cariyaṃ kataṃ karaṇīyaṃ nâparaṃ itthattāyā ti pajānāti*: 'As he thus knows and sees, his mind is freed from the corruption of sensual desire, the corruption of desire for continued existence, the corruption of ignorance. He knows his release as such. He has the insight: "Birth has waned away, the holy life has been led, there is nothing more for thusness." '

The expressions *cittaṃ vimuccati* and *ceto-vimutti* are – given the interchangeability of *citta* and *ceto* referred to above – nothing but the verbal and nominal transformations of each other. Similarly, the verb *pajānāti* corresponds to the noun *paññā*, which is why I have here adopted the rather clumsy phrase 'he has the insight that'. The words *jānato* and *passato* refer to his insights into the four noble truths and the corruptions; they are present participles, so that insight is contemporaneous with *cittaṃ vimuccati*, 'his mind is released'. To make this point I could have stopped the quotation there, but I have quoted the rest of the paragraph both to show that *pajānāti* recurs at the end of it and to make clear that knowing that one is enlightened is a part of being enlightened. Exegetes ancient and modern have dwelt on the distinction between the two; but such texts show that at this stage of Buddhist teaching the one involved the other. This is hardly surprising. One can be in an emotional state, e.g. anxious or depressed, without being clearly aware of it. But since Enlightenment is a state of supreme clarity, 'seeing things as they are', one could not be unclear that one was clear!

* * *

Thus far I have shown that in texts which are generally considered fundamental *ceto-vimutti* and *paññā-vimutti* have the same reference. What I am trying to show to be the later, scholastic interpretation would have enormous difficulty with the wording of the *Mahāvagga* of the *Vinaya Khandhaka*. Here, at the end of the first sermon, the Buddha's final sentence is: *ñāṇam ca pana me dassanaṃ udapādi: akuppā me ceto-vimutti, ayaṃ antimā jāti, n'atthi dāni puna-bbhavo*: 'And the realisation arose in me: the release of my mind is unshakable; this is my last birth, now there is no more rebirth' (Vin I, 11). The last two phrases are a good illustration of redundant synonymity. But the first is the one that most interests us: the Buddha refers to his own Enlightenment as *ceto-vimutti* (which he declares to be irreversible); he does not use at all the term *paññā-vimutti*, which came later to be regarded as hierarchically superior. This seems incompatible with AN I, 61, cited above.

There is even worse trouble for the later interpretation a couple of pages further on in the *Vinaya* narrative. The analytical path stresses the doctrine of the three hallmarks of existence (*ti-lakkhaṇa*), and the *locus classicus* for this doctrine is the *Anatta-lakkhaṇa Sutta*, traditionally considered to have been the Buddha's second sermon. Yet at the end of this sermon, it is said of the five monks to whom it was addressed *anupādāya āsavehi cittāni vimucciṃsu*: 'without grasping, their minds were released from the corruptions' (Vin I, 14). Thus their enlightenment too is referred to as *ceto-vimutti*, even though what directly led to it was what is said in the *Susīma Sutta* (see below p. 124) to lead precisely and exclusively to *paññā-vimutti*.

Ceto-vimutti and *paññā-vimutti* can be used as synonyms also when their parallelism is more expansively expressed. Thus a *sutta* in the *Aṅguttara Nikāya* (*Pañcaka Nipāta, Yodhajīva Vagga, sutta* LXXI) begins as follows: 'Monks, these five things when developed and increased result in release of the mind and bring the benefits of that result, result in release by insight and bring the benefits of that result' (*ceto-vimutti-phalā ca honti ceto-vimutti-phalânisaṃsā ca, paññā-vimutti-phalā ca honti paññā-vimutti-phalânisaṃsā ca*) (AN III, 84-5). The five are perception of the impurity of the body, of the disgusting nature of food, of the unsatisfying character of everything in the world, of the impermanence of all compounded things, and of one's own impending death. The phraseology of the whole *sutta* makes it obvious that *ceto-vimutti* and *paññā-vimutti* are the same. The next *sutta*, AN III, 85-6, is identical, except that here the five things to be developed are perception of impermanence, of the suffering it entails, of the lack of essence in suffering, of abandonment and of dispassion (*anicca-saññā, anicce dukkha-saññā, dukkhe anatta-saññā, pahāna-saññā, virāga-saññā*). This is noteworthy, because the dichotomisers assign perception of impermanence, suffering and lack of self exclusively to *paññā*.

There are a couple of other passages in which *paññā-vimutti* is not contrasted with some other kind of Enlightenment, and so is probably just a term for Enlightenment. Thus SN III, 65-6 (*Khandha-saṃyutta sutta* 58) says that the Buddha is fully released without grasping through his disenchantment with, dispassion for and cessation of each of the five aggregates (named in turn), and a monk released by insight is in just the same case; the difference is only that the Buddha found the way and the others followed. In the *Sutta-nipāta, Māgandiya Sutta* verse 847 says: 'There are no ties for the man who is dispassionate towards his perceptions (*saññā-virattassa*); there are no delusions for the man who is released by insight (*paññā-vimuttassa*). Those who have taken hold of a perception and a view go around in the world clashing.' The *Niddesa* commentary on this passage glosses the *saññā-viratta* as the one who develops the noble path giving priority to calm (*samatha-pubbaṃgamaṃ ariya-maggaṃ bhāveti*), and the *paññā-vimutta* as one who gives priority to insight (*vipassanā*), but makes clear that the goal they reach is the same. This is in accordance with our second interpretation of the two methods, as defined above.

In the texts we have dealt with so far there is no contrast between *ceto-vimutti* and *paññā-vimutti*, nor between a person released by wisdom on the one hand and a person 'released on both sides' (or in any other way) on the other. How did such a contrast arise?

* * *

I believe that the problem begins with the final part of the *Mahā-nidāna Sutta* (DN *sutta* xv), a text best known for its exposition of dependent origination (*paṭicca-samuppāda*). In its final paragraph, this *sutta* has the very formula for the attainment of nirvana which I have discussed above, with the parallelism between *ceto-vimutti* and *paññā-vimutti*. The text – or at least this part of it – thus belongs to what I am considering to be the earliest stratum. The last few paragraphs of the text – the last three pages in the P.T.S. edition – are devoted to several classifications of meditative states, some of which deviate from the standard classifications. It seems to me quite natural that meditative states, internal conditions attained by relatively few people, should be rather difficult to describe, let alone classify, so that in the early stages of a tradition there should be a wide variety of attempts to put those experiences into words. (This leaves open the question to what extent the different descriptions reflect different experiences.)

The *Mahā-nidāna Sutta* (para.33, pp. 68-9) says that there are seven stations of consciousness (*viññāṇa-ṭhiti*) and two planes (*āyatana*). The sixth and seventh stations of consciousness are the formless meditational levels 'plane of the infinity of space' and 'plane of the infinity of consciousness'. (These are familiar from standard listings of the *arūpa-jjhāna*.) The 'two planes' evidently follow on from these; they are the 'plane of being (or beings) without perception' and the 'plane of neither apperception nor lack of it' (*neva-saññā-nâsaññâyatana*, which is in the standard lists). Of each of these nine states the Buddha says (para.34) that one can understand (*pajānāti*) its arising and passing away, its pleasures and risks, and how to get out of it; is it therefore right to be satisfied with it? No, says Ānanda, his interlocutor. Thus each state is being exposed as impermanent and unsatisfactory. At the end of para.34 the Buddha says that a monk who has understood these features of all nine states is released without further grasping (for them) (*anupādā*), and that such a monk is called 'released by wisdom' (*ayaṃ vuccati Ānanda bhikkhu paññā-vimutto*).

This occurrence of the term *paññā-vimutto* could hardly be further from the idea that the person it refers to has not meditated. He has been through all stages of meditation but has understood, in effect, that all of them are impermanent and so unsatisfactory.

In the next paragraph, 35, the Buddha expounds the eight meditational levels called 'releases' (*vimokkhā* – see p. 99 above); they overlap a lot with the previous list, for numbers 4 to 7 are the plane of infinite space, that of infinite consciousness, that of infinite nothingness and that of neither apperception nor the lack of it. The eighth, transcending the rest, is the destruction of apperception and feeling.

The next paragraph, 36, the last in the *sutta*, says that a monk is called *ubhato-bhāga-vimutto*, 'released on both sides', if he can at will attain and leave any of these eight states in any order, and 'through the waning away of the corruptions himself in this very life realises, witnesses, attains and stays in the corruption-free release of mind (*ceto-vimutti*), release by insight (*paññā-vimutti*). There exists no other release on both sides higher or finer than this release on both sides.' This is the climax of the *sutta*.

It is not self-evident what is here meant by 'release on both sides'. The context shows that the referent must be the experience of release undergone by a meditator. This is also the view variously propounded by several passages in the commentaries.[15] Variously, in that they record different opinions about why this is called 'release on both sides'.[16] None of the recorded opinions corresponds to my own guess: that in keeping with the highly redundant style of these texts, 'on both sides' refers to the fact that he can with equal ease enter and leave each state – in the modern idiom, he 'can take it or let it alone'. But even if my guess is right and this is what the term was originally intended to refer to, I suppose we shall never know for sure, and historically it is a dead end, because no ancient text adopted this interpretation.

However, the fact that 'release on both sides' refers to the release of a meditator fits another canonical passage, a succession of three very short and schematic *suttas* (AN, *Navaka Nipāta, Pañcāla Vagga, suttas* XLIII-XLV = AN IV, 451-3).[17] Each of these three short *suttas* has exactly the same pattern. It begins by an anonymous monk asking another anonymous monk, his senior (as one can deduce from the terms of address), what the Buddha meant by a certain term. *Sutta* XLIII deals with the term *kāya-sakkhī*, XLIV with *paññā-vimutto*, XLV with *ubhato-bhāga-vimutto*. These three terms are numbers 3, 2 and 1 on our original list. *Sakkhī* itself means 'eye-witness', so that to add *kāya*, 'body', to it seems redundant. However, what is intended here is that *sakkhī*, in so far as it refers to the eyes, is metaphorical: the explanation of the term shows that the relevant sensation is tactile, or rather perhaps a feeling permeating the body for which there is no term in the vocabulary of sense perception. Our passage simply goes through the standard list of nine meditative attainments (*samāpatti*), starting, as always, from the bottom, and says that one who, achieving and staying in them, touches them with his body is called a *kāya-sakkhī*. But the sting comes in the tail, for it adds that in the first eight cases the Buddha has so

[15] They are listed by I. B. Horner in a footnote (Horner, 1957:151).

[16] See the commentary on this passage, DA II, 514-15.

[17] This passage has been briefly discussed by Gethin, 1992:135-6.

called the meditator metaphorically (*pariyāyena*), but that in the ninth case, the destruction of apperception and feeling, he means it literally (*nippariyāyena*).

Next, the text deals with *paññā-vimutto*. The treatment parallels that of *kāya-sakkhī*. One becomes *paññā-vimutto* as one achieves and stays in each state, and also understands it. This is metaphorical in the first eight cases, literal in the ninth.

The *ubhato-bhāga-vimutto* simply combines the achievements of the *kāya-sakkhī* and the *paññā-vimutto*: he both physically experiences each state (touches it with his body) and, after attaining it, understands it.

This seems to me to be both coherent and at least consistent with the *Mahānidāna Sutta*. Attempts to categorise experiences of meditation are unlikely to be very successful, so that it is not surprising if one remains puzzled by the difference between touching a state with the body and merely 'achieving and staying in' that state. This unclarity may well explain why some of the commentaries cited by Horner (see note 15) give *ubhato*, 'both', a different referent, and say that one is released both from the material (*rūpa*) levels and the immaterial (*arūpa*) levels, also called *nāma*. But the main point for our line of inquiry is that in none of the passages so far cited is there any implication that release without meditation is laudable or even possible: quite the contrary. So how did this view of the *paññā-vimutto* as a meditator get stood on its head?

* * *

At this point we turn to the *Susīma Sutta* (SN, *Nidāna-saṃyutta, Mahāvagga dasamaṃ* = XII, 70 = SN II, 119-128). As mentioned above, I need to devote a separate article to this text, since I wish to demonstrate that it is an incoherent reworking of a text which originally made quite different points. This original text, or something like it, is preserved in Chinese translation. In that version (which is too long to reproduce here) Susīma, an intelligent non-Buddhist renunciate of some kind, gets into the

Buddhist Order because he wants to discover the secret of the Buddhists' success with the public. He spends the first fortnight picking up the rudiments of what is being taught, so that he has some idea of what Enlightenment should consist of. A newcomer, he is not socially integrated into the group of monks in that monastery. One of them, to put him down, says that all of them are already Enlightened. Susīma, who has learnt what this should involve, cross-examines the monk, who is immediately shown up: he cannot even claim that they are free of greed and hatred. Susīma then betakes himself to the Buddha, who realises – perhaps because he is aware of the preceding conversation – that Susīma shows promise. The Buddha then teaches him the chain of dependent origination.[18] On receiving this teaching, Susīma naturally makes some spiritual progress, and the result – indeed the outward sign – of this progress is that he confesses to having entered the Order as a spy. The Buddha then commends him and the text ends by implying that Susīma is now headed towards further spiritual improvement.

It is not difficult to see why the above text should have got changed: it is most uncomplimentary to a group of monks. There are quite a few stories in the Canon about monks' stupidity, incompetence, etc., but they seem to be virtually confined to the *Vinaya* or at least to originate in a strictly *vinaya* context.[19] From such a *vinaya* context they could not be removed, because in those stories it is the shortcomings of monks which occasion what the Buddha does next, whether it be promulgating a rule or retiring to the Pārileyyaka forest (Vin I, 352ff.).

In the Pali version, Susīma asks the monks who claim to be Enlightened whether they have attained the first five super-knowledges (*abhiññā*) as they are listed, for example, in the

[18] This must be an original feature of the text, because it is in the *Nidāna-saṃyutta*, which is precisely a collection of texts dealing with this topic.

[19] For example, the story of Ariṭṭha, who saw nothing wrong in sexual intercourse for monks, begins the *Alagaddūpama Sutta* (MN *sutta* 22) but presumably originates in the *Vinaya* context where it is also found (Vin IV, 135; Vin II, 25-8).

Sāmañña-phala Sutta (DN I, 77-84). They say no. He then asks whether they have touched with their bodies and stay in those tranquil releases which are formless, transcending forms. (This is the very wording we have encountered in the definitions in the *Kīṭāgiri Sutta.*) No, they say, they have not: 'we are released by insight'. (The commentary (SA II, 126-7) glosses this: *Mayaṃ nijjhānakā sukkha-vipassakā, paññā-matten' eva vimuttā ti*: 'We are meditation-less "dry intuiters", released by insight alone.') Susīma, puzzled, asks them to explain, but they refuse, so he asks the Buddha. The Buddha says that if you know the way things are (which refers to dependent origination) you know nirvana. He then gives Susīma an abbreviated version of the *Anatta-lakkhaṇa Sutta*, showing that each of the five *khandha* is impermanent, unsatisfactory and not the self, and that realisation of this leads to dispassion and so to release. Then he teaches Susīma the chain of dependent origination (as in the Chinese) and asks him if he sees it. Susīma says he does (p. 126). At this the Buddha asks Susīma the same six questions as Susīma put to the monks, and Susīma agrees that he is not having any of those super-normal experiences. The Buddha does not then tell Susīma that he is Enlightened, but the commentary (SA II, 127) draws the conclusion that he is, a natural deduction if one takes the monks' claim seriously. Susīma then confesses to being there under false pretenses; the Buddha replies that it is a very serious crime, but a good thing he has confessed: he may now make further progress. (But if he were already Enlightened, what progress could he still make?)

In this summary I have glossed over some of the anomalies in the text, and I hope to examine them all elsewhere; here I deal only with the most important. The text itself (unlike the commentary and despite de La Vallée Poussin's report [1936-7:202]) does not claim that Susīma attained Enlightenment just by understanding a sermon, but certainly the monks make that claim, after Susīma has forced them to admit, under cross-examination, that they have no meditative accomplishments. It is in any case a *vinaya* offence (*pācittiya* 8, Vin IV, 25) to claim that one is

Enlightened, even if it is true.[20] In this case, comparison with the Chinese version shows, I believe, that they are lying.

The redactor of our Pali text wanted to change the story so that the monks already with the Buddha became clearly superior to the newcomer from a non-Buddhist sect. So their Enlightenment had to be genuine, and his questions simply questions, not a clever cross-examination. At the same time, the things the Enlightened monks had *not* achieved could hardly be as basic as the elimination of greed and hatred. For these the redactor substituted the supernormal powers listed in the *Sāmañña-phala Sutta*. This was an intelligent choice, in that the Buddha had suggested that the exercise of supernormal powers was unnecessary, even distasteful. The redactor did not go as far back along the standard path as to deny the four *jhāna* (in textual terms: *Sāmañña-phala* paras. 75-81); but that step was taken by the commentary.[21] Presumably the implication anyone would draw from a lack of super-knowledges (*abhiññā*) was that the meditative attainments which bestow those powers had not been reached. So the monks seem to claim Enlightenment without having meditated.

The redactor has now made the monks present Susīma with a conundrum. He is naturally puzzled and resorts to the Buddha. The Buddha has to show Susīma, in this new version, that what the monks claim is indeed possible: that is why he puts Susīma through the same questions as Susīma put to the monks. And it is probably not arbitrary that the redactor chose the *Anatta-lakkhaṇa Sutta* (Vin I, 14) as his interpolation to demonstrate the

[20] The *Vinaya* context suggests that the prohibition was originally directed mainly against informing laity, but I understand that by tradition it is interpreted generally.

[21] Lance Cousins emphasised this point at the seminar. In his view, all the canonical texts assume (even if they do not state explicitly) that attainment of the four *jhāna* is a pre-requisite not merely for Enlightenment but even for stream-entry. He disagrees with the third sentence of this chapter, for he thinks that the change originated in the commentaries, and that this marks a break in the tradition. He may be right, though I am sceptical whether it will ever be possible to settle the matter so precisely. In any case I have shown that there was a multi-stranded debate and that the *suttas* themselves bear ample witness to a devaluation of concentration by some monks.

supremacy of *paññā*; or that the commentator had Susīma achieve Enlightenment as soon as he had heard it. By tradition, this was the second sermon the Buddha preached to the five monks who were his first disciples, and on hearing it all five of them achieved Enlightenment (see p. 118 above). Thus, according to the Buddha's standard biography, this was the first recorded case of Enlightenment being achieved as the result of listening to a sermon! The analogy is not really valid, because of course the five monks had been through years of preparation for this moment.

In this case I think that the redefinition of *paññā-vimutti* to exclude meditation has arisen not as the result of debate but rather as a kind of narrative accident due to Sangha apologetics. But I cannot exclude the possibility that the author of the Pali *Susīma Sutta* that has come down to us had views on the matter to put forward. What I do however feel rather sure of is that he had no sound authority for those views. So he may have tried, albeit obliquely, to cite the preaching of the *Anatta-lakkhaṇa Sutta* as a precedent.

* * *

The *Susīma Sutta* seems to me to have been directly challenged.[22] That challenge is contained in the *sutta* which gave de La Vallée Poussin the title for his article, for it contrasts the spiritual attainments of two monks, Musīla and Nārada. Unfortunately de La Vallée Poussin did not notice that the message of this *sutta* directly contradicts that of the *Susīma Sutta*. It is SN, *Nidāna-saṃyutta, Mahāvagga aṭṭhamam* = XII, 68 = SN II, 115-8; in the present arrangement of the Pali Canon it stands almost

[22] Of course, this can only be true if the present Pali *Susīma Sutta* already existed when this *sutta* was composed. Otherwise the course of development must have been more complicated and cannot be precisely traced; but we can still deduce debate. We are dealing with texts orally composed and preserved, so that when a new version is inserted in one recitation tradition it does not necessarily oust the old version everywhere.

immediately before the *Susīma Sutta* but in the Chinese version of the *Saṃyukta Āgama* it follows shortly after it.

This *sutta* is only three pages long but has a fairly complex narrative structure, in which four monks figure. First Saviṭṭha puts some questions to Musīla. He asks him whether he knows and sees the chain of dependent origination for himself, as opposed to in any way taking it on trust. Musīla says he does. This interchange is repeated for each link in the chain, taken positively (decrepitude and death arise because of birth) and negatively (decrepitude and death cease when birth ceases). After this comes the proposition 'the cessation of becoming is nirvana' (*bhava-nirodho nibbānaṃ*) (p. 117, paras. 26-7). This too Musīla knows and sees for himself. Thereupon Saviṭṭha says, 'So the Ven. Musīla is an *arahant*; his corruptions have waned away.' Musīla is silent, so one assumes agreement.

We have already met Saviṭṭha: he was the proponent of 'release by faith'. This is the only other place in the Canon where he occurs; the significance of this may be that he represents faith – taking teachings on trust – and is thus the perfect foil to Musīla.

Nārada then asks Saviṭṭha to ask him the same questions as he asked Musīla. He does, and the same lengthy interchange takes place, culminating in 'the cessation of becoming is nirvana'. But when Saviṭṭha asks Nārada if he is an *arahant* he replies, 'With full insight (*sammā-paññāya*[23]) I have correctly seen the truth: that the cessation of becoming is nirvana. And yet I am not an arahant. My corruptions have not waned away.' He continues by comparing himself to a hot and thirsty traveller who sees water in a well but cannot reach it: he might have knowledge of the water but could not touch it physically (*udakan ti kho ñāṇam assa na ca kāyena phusitvā vihareyya*).

Finally there is a third, brief conversation: between Saviṭṭha and Ānanda. The latter asks Saviṭṭha what he has to say about Nārada, and he replies, 'Nothing but good.'

[23] The P.T.S. *sammapaññāya* is a misprint.

In this text Nārada, whose words are evidently approved, interprets *paññā* in the narrow sense of intellection without a deeper, experiential realisation – an interpretation that the Pali *Susīma Sutta* would justify – and denies that it is an adequate method for achieving Enlightenment. Of course he must be right, otherwise every student who learnt the chain of dependent origination for her exams would thereby be Enlightened! Nārada does not use the term *kāya-sakkhī* but we have seen that the phrase 'physically touching' (*kāyena phusitvā*) is its equivalent.

* * *

The *Susīma Sutta*'s formulations, combined with the concept of *ubhato-bhāga-vimutto*, have led directly to the top three types in our original list. But not only to that. At SN I, 191 distinctions seem to multiply in a mysterious manner. The setting is a *pavāraṇā*, the ceremony at the end of the rains retreat in which the monks who have passed that period together ask each other forgiveness if they have offended in any way. The text begins (p. 190) by saying that all the five hundred monks present are *arahant*s, so it is not surprising that the Buddha tells Sāriputta that he finds nothing to criticise in any of them. He says that sixty of them have the three knowledges (*tevijjā*), sixty have the six super-knowledges (*chaḷabhiññā*), sixty are released on both sides and the rest released by insight.[24] Since one acquires the six super-knowledges by meditation, it can be deduced that these are meditators. This text therefore does not agree with our list of types, but rather gives what I have labelled the third interpretation of the two paths to Enlightenment: that they are alternatives. (The presence of the term 'released on both sides' must imply the third or the fourth interpretation, since it presupposes that a release which is *not* on both sides is possible.) However, the presence of

[24] The commentary (SA I, 278) gives no help. It glosses neither *tevijjā* nor *chaḷabhiññā*. It here explains *ubhato-bhāga* as *nāma* and *rūpa*.

monks with the three knowledges as a separate category baffles me. The three knowledges are those of one's former lives, of the rebirths of all beings, and of the four noble truths plus that one's corruptions have gone. According to those texts in which they are described, such as the *Sāmañña-phala Sutta* (DN I, 81-4), they are an invariable concomitant of Enlightenment. Since the commentator too was apparently stumped by this category, I can only resort to the explanation of last resort: that the text is either corrupt, *tevijjā* having crept in from a marginal gloss after it was written down, or compiled with extreme carelessness.

No such explanations are called for in the case of the last text we have to deal with, AN III, 355-6 = *Chakka Nipāta, Dhammika Vagga, sutta* XLVI. This is the text summarised by de La Vallée Poussin at the outset of his article (see Appendix). It is important to note that the *sutta* has no Chinese version, which strongly suggests that it is a late addition to the corpus. This *sutta* adheres to the third interpretation of the two paths to Enlightenment – that there are two valid methods – and in this respect is less extreme than the *Kītāgiri Sutta* and our list. But it does spell out that one does not have to be a meditator to achieve Enlightenment.

The text is a sermon attributed to a monk called Mahā Cunda. Though the commentary (AA III, 379) says he was Sāriputta's younger brother, the lack of a Chinese version casts grave doubt on this. Mahā Cunda preaches to some monks that they fall into two groups, which he refers to as *dhamma-yogā* and *jhāyī*. The latter are clearly meditators; the former term is not found elsewhere in the Canon, but seems to mean 'whose discipline is the teaching'; the commentary glosses it as *dhamma-kathika*, 'preacher'. The reference must be to monks who work purely intellectually. These two sets of monks are on bad terms and complain about each other. Mahā Cunda tells them to be reconciled. The academic types should praise the meditators, because 'rare are those who touch the deathless state with their bodies and stay there' (*ye amataṃ dhātuṃ kāyena phusitvā viharanti*). And the meditators should praise the academics, because 'rare are those who penetrate to the profound goal of truth and see it' (*ye gambhīram attha-padaṃ ativijjha passanti*).

This *sutta* shows that before the Pali Canon (specifically, the *Aṅguttara Nikāya*) was completely closed, the change in doctrine had had its effect on behaviour, and monks, in one place at least – and no doubt more widely – really did divide into meditators and non-meditators.

* * *

It may be possible to suggest equally or more plausible alternatives to the precise line of development which we have traced. We claim, however, to have demonstrated in this paper:

1. that Enlightenment without meditation was probably never envisaged by the Buddha or in the earliest texts, and that the term *paññā-vimutti* originally did not refer to it;

2. that *paññā-vimutti* came to refer to Enlightenment without meditation (or at least without certain specific meditational attainments) and that this change may well have had something to do with the changing of the *Susīma Sutta*;

3. that in the end, as generally acknowledged, there were indeed groups of monks in the Pali tradition who left meditation to others, without renouncing the quest for Enlightenment.

* * *

Can we say anything about the chronology of these changes?

In introducing his paraphrase of the *Kīṭāgiri Sutta*, Kurt Schmidt (1989:201) draws attention to terms in our list which he calls 'abhidhamma terms' and says that they show that the text must be several centuries later than the Buddha; he also points out that the terms recur in the *Bhaddāli Sutta* (MN *sutta* 65 = MN I, 437-447). By calling them *abhidhamma* terms he may be putting the cart before the horse, and his 'several centuries' is surely a wild guess. However, his note is valuable in drawing attention to the close relationship between the *Kīṭāgiri* and the *Bhaddāli Suttas*. For both deal primarily with the Buddha's introducing the rule that a monk should not eat an evening meal; and in the *Bhaddāli Sutta* he explains that formerly monks did not need so many rules, but now monks are no longer what they used to be, so they need stricter regulation. This confirms what is implied by the development we have traced: that texts with our list of seven types do not belong to the earliest stratum.

This tells one next to nothing about absolute chronology. But it is hardly likely that monks who were educated to think that Enlightenment required meditation would later in life have changed that view by accepting the narrow interpretation of *paññā-vimutti*. For such a change in the soteriology, a whole turnover of monastic personnel seems required, a matter of at least two to three generations. I suppose the minimum time span that would be required would be the same as that between the Buddha's death and the Second Communal Recitation, for at that event there were still a tiny number of participants who had known the Buddha personally. I have calculated elsewhere (Gombrich, 1988a:17) that that would be about 65 years. That represents the minimum. Because of the similarities between the *Vinayas* and the collections of *suttas* preserved by the different schools, it is hard to think that those texts were not largely put together by the time of Asoka's missions and the great expansion of Buddhism, about 150 years after the parinirvana (Gombrich, 1992a); but this does not preclude some changes and interpolations, to say nothing of corruptions.

* * *

Throughout this chapter I have referred to Buddhist salvation indifferently as nirvana and Enlightenment. The two terms, so far as the early texts are concerned, are perfect synonyms. Nirvana (Pali: *nibbāna*) means 'blowing out', and refers to the blowing out of the fires of greed, hatred and delusion. Enlightenment, which translates *bodhi* (literally 'awakening'), refers to the same thing, but in meaning it identifies the gnostic rather than the emotional side of the achievement.

We have seen a tendency to dichotomise and to assign the control of the emotions ('calm' (*samatha*)) to the method of achieving the goal by meditation, whereas the understanding of reality is assigned to the intellectual method. We have also seen a tendency (not the same tendency, but overlapping in many instances) to accord the intellectual method the higher value, even to the extent of casting doubt on the total efficacy of meditation. The final result is Theravādin monks who strive for Enlightenment without meditating.

I know of no evidence for non-meditators in the early Mahāyāna. On the other hand, there is a pronounced tendency, for instance in the *Lotus Sūtra*, to define the religious goal in gnostic terms, as *bodhi/sambodhi* (see p. 66). Of course, the Mahāyāna defined itself primarily in ethical terms: one should aim to become a *bodhisattva* because it was not good enough to strive only for one's own salvation without saving others. Moreover, Mahāyāna texts are so heterogeneous that it is difficult to generalise about them. Nevertheless, the very title of a large corpus of early Mahāyāna literature, the *prajñā-pāramitā*, shows that to some extent the historian may extrapolate the trend to extol insight, *prajñā* at the expense of dispassion, *virāga*, the control of the emotions. Such extrapolation, however, is another story.

APPENDIX

Translation of Louis de La Vallée Poussin: 'Musīla et Nārada: Le Chemin de Nirvāṇa', first part, beginning at the second paragraph (pp. 189-92).

Without being too rash, one may discriminate in the Buddhist sources, both ancient and scholastic, between two opposed theories, the same as the *Bhagavadgītā* distinguishes by the names of *sāṃkhya* and *yoga*: the theory which makes salvation a purely or mainly intellectual achievement, and the theory which makes salvation the goal of ascetic and ecstatic disciplines.

On the one hand we have *prajñā*, 'discrimination between things' (*dharma-pravicaya*); *pratisaṃkhyāna*, discrimination; *vipaśyanā*, 'contemplation'; seeing the four noble truths (*satya-darśana*); application to the doctrine (compare *dhamma-yoga*, AN III, 355). The ascetic recognises things for what they are (*yathābhūtam*): painful, impermanent, empty, without self; he is disgusted with them; he kills desire and as a result stops the process of acts bringing retribution and of transmigration.

On the other hand, the path of *śamatha*, 'calm': of *samādhi*, 'concentration'; of the *dhyānas* and the *samāpattis*, ecstasies and contemplations; of *bhāvanā*, 'meditation'. By a gradual purification and the gradual suppression of ideas (*saṃkalpa*), this path leads up to a state of unconsciousness – cessation of all forms of thought, *saṃjñāvedayitanirodha* or just *nirodhasamāpatti* – which puts the ascetic in touch with a transcendent reality which is Nirvāṇa (ancient doctrine) or is like Nirvāṇa (Sarvāstivādin scholasticism). In principle, if not in fact, this path has nothing specifically Buddhist about it; 'seeing the truths' has no place in it; speculative understanding (*prajñā*) is not employed in it ....

[Here de La Vallée Poussin summarises AN III, 355-6; see p. 130 above.]

For both, salvation – the end of transmigration, the cessation of the contingent and the mortal, entry into the permanent and immortal – depends on achieving Nirvāṇa. One side holds that one must by contemplation come into physical contact with Nirvāṇa; the others think that it is enough to realise Nirvāṇa intellectually.

V

Who was Aṅgulimāla?

Few Buddhist stories can be better known than that of Aṅgulimāla, the brigand who wore a necklace[1] of his victims' fingers, from which he derived his name. According to the version generally known to Buddhists, he needed a thousand victims, and was just one short when he had a chance to complete his tally by killing the Buddha. The Buddha was walking through the forest where Aṅgulimāla waylaid his victims, so he tried to attack him, but although he ran as fast as he could and the Buddha seemed to walk at normal speed, he could not catch up with him. At this miracle, Aṅgulimāla spoke to the Buddha, and after a brief dialogue in verse declared himself converted.

The Buddha converts Aṅgulimāla by one of the commonest of his skilful means: playing upon words. In this case, he puns not on a technical term but on a very common verb, *tiṭṭhati*, meaning to stay or stop. The brigand in the opening verse of the exchange gives this its physical meaning; the Buddha in his reply ethicises the term, and thus resolves an apparent paradox. This so impresses the brigand that he declares himself converted.

There are two texts about this episode in the Pali Canon. In the *Thera-gāthā* (*Thag*) there is a set of 26 verses (866-91) ascribed to Aṅgulimāla. The first five of these verses correspond to the set of five verses which occurs in the *Aṅgulimāla Sutta* (*AS*) (MN II, 97-105) at the nub of the above episode. All but the last five of the rest of the *Thag* verses occur at the end of the *AS*, where they are described as a pronouncement (*udāna*) uttered by Aṅgulimāla on attaining Enlightenment. They will not concern me further

[1] *Mālā* is usually translated 'garland', but here 'necklace' may bring the point home better. The texts call Aṅgulimāla a *cora*, which is usually translated 'thief' or 'robber', but in this case the emphasis on violence rather than stealing (which indeed is never mentioned) suggests that 'brigand' is a more appropriate translation.

here. Nor shall I be concerned with the famous episode which follows Aṅgulimāla's conversion in the *AS*, when he encounters a women who is undergoing a difficult labour and saves the lives of mother and baby by saying, as an act of truth, that he has never consciously deprived a living creature of life since he was born in his noble birth, i.e., joined the Buddhist Order. This statement, known as the *Aṅgulimāla paritta*, is still used in Buddhist Sri Lanka to help women in labour (Gombrich, 1971:224). The episode derives its point from the contrast between the now guaranteed harmlessness of the Buddhist monk and his former career as a mass murderer.

But who exactly was this mass murderer? We are told in the *AS* (p. 102) the names of his parents, Gārgya and Mantāṇī, and can deduce from them that he was a brahmin. But why did he wear a necklace of fingers? Although the answer to this and related questions is quite well known among Buddhists, what they know is derived from the Pali commentaries. Moreover, when we scrutinise those commentaries, they turn out to be fairly incoherent. The *Thag* lacks a prose narrative, so at this point in our inquiry it is not relevant. What does the *AS* have to say? Its simple description of Aṅgulimāla is presented in its opening lines. 'At that time in the kingdom of King Pasenadi of Kosala there was a brigand called Aṅgulimāla. He was ferocious, bloody-handed, addicted to slaughter, merciless towards living creatures. He annihilated villages, towns, country districts. As he kept on killing people, he wore a necklace of their fingers.' One day, after eating a meal he had begged in Sāvatthi, the Buddha was on his way and about to cross Aṅgulimāla's path. The locals warned him off. They repeated the description of Aṅgulimāla, and said that people only made that trip in large groups, and even so Aṅgulimāla would get them. The Buddha continued undeterred. When the brigand saw him coming on alone, he determined to kill him and armed himself in preparation.

In this account the only motive that Aṅgulimāla has for trying to kill the Buddha is sheer bloody-mindedness. Granted, he is a robber. But the Buddha, as he could see at a glance, is a renunciate and has nothing he could steal. So what is he up to?

If the only point of this episode is to serve as a preamble to the saving of a woman in labour, it might put the contrast between a monk's harmlessness and his former cruelty at its starkest if his motives had been purely sadistic. But this seems rather too thin, especially as an explanation for the necklace of fingers. It did not satisfy the tradition, and the commentators supplied a full background story.

* * *

There are two commentaries: that on the MN, the *Papañca-sūdanī* (*Ps*), which is ascribed to Buddhaghosa, and that on the *Thag*, part of the *Paramattha-dīpanī* (*Pad*), which is ascribed to Dhammapāla. The *Ps* text (III, 328-31) seems to be somewhat corrupt, and Horner's P.T.S. edition is not a good one: both her punctuation and her choice of readings suggest that she did not understand the text very well. Nevertheless, I shall use the P.T.S. editions of all the texts discussed, because they are the most widely accessible.

The relevant part of the *Pad* as edited for the P.T.S. by Woodward (III, 54-6) is also imperfect. In some of the glosses, Dhammapāla's text is so close to Buddhaghosa's that he must either have copied the *Ps* or written a paraphrase. Since it is very close but not identical, it looks as if he may have had a version of the older text which was less corrupt; possibly we might call it a different recension. However, in the narrative passage that we are about to discuss Dhammapāla seems rather to be retelling in his own words the story told by Buddhaghosa and making some effort to iron out inconsistencies.

In the following summary of the story, sentences in the first three paragraphs which are not preceded by *Ps* or *Pad* summarise what is common to both versions; sentences preceded by *Ps* summarise what is only in Buddhaghosa's version; and sentences preceded by *Pad* summarise what is only in Dhammapāla's version. After the first three paragraphs the divergences increase, so I have simply alternated paragraphs giving the *Ps* version with paragraphs giving the *Pad* version.

Aṅgulimāla was born a brahmin, son of the chaplain to the king of Kosala. He was born at night, and at the time of his birth all the weapons in the city shone brightly. The king saw his own weapons flash and was frightened. Aṅgulimāla's father observed that he had been born under the constellation of thieves. He attended on the king in the morning to ask how he had slept, and the king told him of his misgivings. The chaplain said that he had had a son who was destined to be a brigand. The king asked him whether he would operate alone or *Ps*: harass the realm / *Pad*: lead a band. The chaplain said he would operate solo; he asked if the king wanted him killed. The king said a solo performer could be allowed to live. *Ps*: They called him Ahiṃsaka, 'Harmless', because the king's weapons hurt no one when they flashed. *Pad*: They called him Hiṃsaka, 'Harmful', because his birth worried the king, but later that got changed to Ahiṃsaka.

At this point *Pad* says he grew up to be as strong as seven elephants, and explains this by an episode in a previous life when he made a fire at which a *paccekabuddha*[2] dried his rain-drenched clothes.

He was sent to Taxila for his education. He was his teacher's best pupil and the others became jealous. They hatched a plot to set the teacher against him. They managed to persuade the teacher that Aṅgulimāla was treacherously deceiving him: the implication is that he was having an affair with the teacher's wife. The teacher wanted to kill him in revenge but felt he could not do so directly. *Ps*: He thought it would ruin his business if he were known to have killed his own pupil. *Pad*: He was too strong for anyone to kill, except by a stratagem. So the teacher asked

[2] A *paccekabuddha* is a person in a mythical category: he has attained Enlightenment without the benefit of learning of the/a Buddha's teachings, and does not himself teach.

Aṅgulimāla for the present which by custom a pupil must give his teacher at the end of his training. *Ps*: He asked him to kill a thousand legs [*sic*: *jaṅghā*, which usually refers to the leg from the knee to the ankle]. *Pad*: He asked him to bring a thousand fingers from people's right hands. He thought that someone would be sure to kill Aṅgulimāla while resisting. *Ps*: Aṅgulimāla protested that he was born in a family who did no harm, but his teacher said that without the concluding gift what he had learnt would prove fruitless. *Pad*: Aṅgulimāla summoned up the hard-heartedness he had long been cultivating.

Ps: Then he killed people in the middle of the jungle, or where they entered or left it; he took none of their clothes, but just tried to keep count of them; however, he lost count because murderers have confused thoughts. Then he cut a finger off each, and kept them, but the fingers were getting lost from the store. So he pierced them and made a necklace out of them. That is how he came to be called Aṅgulimāla.

Pad: Then he lived on a hill-top, from where he could espy travellers. He went and took their fingers [the text does not say that he killed them] and hung the fingers on a tree. But vultures and crows ate some, and others fell to the ground and rotted. So the tally was not being made up. But he threaded the fingers on a string to make a necklace and wore it like a sacrificial thread.[3] So he got the name Aṅgulimāla.

Ps: So nobody could enter the forest. In his search for victims, Aṅgulimāla entered villages by night, kicked down the doors and murdered people in their beds. So people left the villages for towns, and the towns for the cities, till everyone from three leagues around had abandoned their homes and encamped round the royal court in Sāvatthi. There they complained to the king.

Pad: People stopped travelling, so he killed them in the villages. In due course everyone migrated from the area. At this point Aṅgulimāla was one finger short of his thousand. People told the

[3] For *yaññopacitaṃ* read *yaññopavītaṃ*.

King of Kosala, so he had an announcement made, proclaiming that he would soon catch the brigand and summoning his forces.

Ps: Then the brahmin realised, and told his wife, that this Aṅgulimāla was their son Harmless. She asked him to bring the lad home but he said he did not dare. Thereupon she went out herself to fetch him. That morning the Buddha saw Aṅgulimāla (with his divine eye) and realised that if he went to meet him he would be saved: on hearing a single verse recited in the forest he would take ordination and realise the six super-knowledges. But if he failed to go, Aṅgulimāla would sin against his mother (i.e., kill her) and become unsavable. So the Buddha decided to favour Aṅgulimāla. After finishing his meal, he set out.

Pad: Aṅgulimāla's mother heard the proclamation and told her husband that it was their son; he should go and reprimand him and bring him home, otherwise the king would have him killed. The father replied that he had no use for such a son; let the king do as he pleased. Aṅgulimāla's mother went out herself to fetch him. The Buddha saw that Aṅgulimāla was (potentially) in his last life, whereas if he met his mother he would kill her for the thousandth finger; so after his meal he went the thirty leagues to that forest on foot.

Ps: At that time Aṅgulimāla was fed up with his poor food and living conditions, and had killed 999 people. When he realised that he needed only one more, he decided to kill the next person he saw. Then he would have paid for his training. After that he would have his beard trimmed, take a bath, change clothes, and go to see his parents. So he came from the middle of the jungle to its edge. And there he saw the Buddha.

Pad: Just as the Buddha arrived at the forest, Aṅgulimāla spotted his mother at a distance, and thought, 'Today I'll kill my mother and get the missing finger.' So he drew his sword and ran after her. The Buddha interposed himself between them. When Aṅgulimāla saw him, he thought, 'Why kill my mother for that finger? Let her live. I'll kill this renunciate and take his.' So he drew his sword and followed the Buddha.

At this point both commentaries rejoin the text (the *AS* and *Thag* respectively). The texts concerning this episode make no mention of any mother; in the *AS* the mere names of Aṅgulimāla's parents occur later. The *AS* says that Aṅgulimāla chases the Buddha as fast as he can, but to his amazement cannot catch him, though he is walking normally. So he stops, and calls on the Buddha to stop. The Buddha replies, 'I have stopped. Aṅgulimāla; you stop too.' Aṅgulimāla replies in a verse (which is also the first of his verses in the *Thag*):

> 'While going, you say, renunciate, "I have stopped", and me,
> who have stopped, you call "not stopped".
> I ask you this, renunciate: How have you stopped
> and I not stopped?'

The Buddha replies:

> 'I have stopped, Aṅgulimāla,
> by forever renouncing violence against all creatures.
> You are unrestrained towards living beings.
> So I have stopped and you have not stopped.'

The next verse, the third in the sequence of five which constitute the climax to this episode, is extremely problematic and the crux of this article. Before tackling it, let me review the story told in the commentaries.

Buddhaghosa prefaces the story in the *Ps* with these words: 'It says in the text that he is wearing a necklace of fingers. Why? Because his teacher told him to. This is the background story.'

On this crucial point the story is not very satisfactory. The motive behind its origination seems to be to show that basically Aṅgulimāla, who later turned into a peaceful monk and achieved Enlightenment, was a thoroughly good person, who only acted as he did in order to obey his teacher. Indeed, before he got into trouble with his teacher (through no fault of his own) his name was Harmless!

According to Buddhaghosa, he is explicitly ordered to kill a thousand people (though I do not understand why the text refers to them as a thousand legs), and the fingers come in later as a mere counting device. Dhammapāla evidently found this too absurd and tried to make the teacher ask him directly for fingers. Even he, however, was not very successful at achieving coherence, if the text is to be trusted, because a thousand fingers from right hands could be supplied by two hundred people, and getting them would not necessarily involve killing. Both versions then resort to a ludicrous account of why the brigand decided to wear the fingers round his neck. No one considers how vast and bulky a necklace of a thousand fingers would be.

Obviously we do not expect from such sources a story which has verisimilitude, but we do expect somewhat more coherence.

* * *

In the *suttas* of the four *nikāyas*, i.e., the canonical collections of sermons, the Buddha occasionally interacts with super-normal beings. But for the most part he interacts with, and in particular preaches to, human beings, and they seem to be realistically portrayed by our modern criteria of realism. For example, among the 34 *suttas* of the *Dīgha Nikāya*, just five – the *Janavasabha*, the *Mahāgovinda*, *Mahāsamaya*, *Sakkapañha* and *Āṭānāṭiya* – are preached to or by gods, but they are also concerned mainly or exclusively with gods, and so clearly fall into a category distinct from most of the Buddha's sermons; T.W. Rhys Davids, reasonably, calls them 'mythological' (Rhys Davids, 1910:294). (They overlap with another distinct category, a group of *suttas* which deal with rebirth; overlap, in that the *Janavasabha* and *Mahāgovinda* have elements of both.[4]) If we except this clearly defined 'mythological group', none of the Buddha's interlocutors

[4] The other members of this group are the *Mahāpadāna* and *Mahāsudassana Suttas*.

seem to do anything which, to our way of thinking, they could not possibly have done.

One can go further, once one has defined what would have struck the Buddha's followers as a realistic account. They accepted that by ascetic or meditative practices people could attain certain super-normal powers called *iddhi* or *iddhi-pāṭihāriya*. These powers are listed, for example, in the *Kevaddha Sutta* (DN I, 212); and the Buddha there makes the point that there is a kind of magic (*vijjā*) which can produce the same effects: they have no religious value. He goes on to say the same about the ability to read other people's thoughts. The Buddha's human interlocutors in the *Dīgha Nikāya* do not in fact display any such powers, but even if they did, that would not have appeared unrealistic to the Buddha's followers, the earliest audiences of these texts.

There also occur, in parts of the Pali Canon generally regarded as old, accounts of Buddhist monks performing miracles (*pāṭihāriya*) which fall outside the standard list of *iddhi*. For example, the monk Dabba, who had attained Enlightenment at the age of seven, had a luminous finger by the light of which he would conduct monks who arrived after dark to their lodgings (Vin III, 159-60); and Aṅgulimāla's saving of the woman in childbirth in our texts might be assigned to the same category. The fact that to the modern reader a more naturalistic explanation might present itself is not relevant; we are concerned with how reality appeared to the authors and early audiences of the texts.

The Buddha's interlocutors mainly fall into two categories: laymen (often brahmins) and ascetics. Some of the latter have striking practices. In the *Pāṭika Sutta* (DN *sutta* xxiv) we hear of a naked ascetic, a nobleman called Kora (*Korakhattiyo*), who behaves just like a dog, going naked on all fours and eating from the ground with his mouth, not using his hands (DN III, 6); and of another naked ascetic who restricts his movements but lives only on meat and strong drink, never taking rice (DN III, 9). The Buddha addresses one of the *suttas* of the *Majjhima Nikāya* (57: *Kukkuravatika Sutta*) to another man, Seniya, who lived like a dog, and a man called Puṇṇa who lived like a cow. The Buddha says that if they succeed in their vows they will be reborn as a dog and a cow respectively; if they fail, they will go to hell (MN I, 388-9).

What I am trying to show is that, unless the *AS* is unique, Aṅgulimāla must have been a type of person recognizable in the environment of his day. No doubt there were various fearsome brigands around; but did they wear garlands of fingers? If so, why? The commentators seem not to have any plausible answers.

At this point let us return to the text.

* * *

The next verse is printed in the P.T.S. edition (by Chalmers) of the MN as follows:

> cirassaṃ vata me mahito mahesi
> mahāvanaṃ samaṇoyaṃ paccavādi
> so 'haṃ cirassā pahāssaṃ pāpaṃ
> sutvāna gāthaṃ tava dhammayuttaṃ.

Like the verses that precede and follow it, this verse is supposed to be in the *tuṭṭhubha* metre, with eleven syllables per line. Yet the first *pāda* has ten syllables, the second twelve (without being the permitted variant, a *jagatī*), the third again only ten. Clearly the text is corrupt.

For the second *pāda*, the P.T.S. editor records the following variants. Burmese MS: *mahāvanaṃ pāpuṇi saccavādi*; Siamese printed edition: *mahāvanaṃ samaṇa paccupādi*; Sinhala MSS: *mahāvana* (misprint for *mahāvanaṃ*?) *samaṇo 'yaṃ paccupādi*. The reading *paccavādi* is attested only in the Burmese text of the *Ps*; the P.T.S. editor must have chosen it as *lectio difficilior*. In the P.T.S. edition of the *Thag*, the second *pāda* reads *mahāvanaṃ samaṇo paccupādi*; this, like the Burmese variant, would at least scan.

In the *Thag*, the third *pāda* also scans:

so 'ham cajissāmi sahassapāpaṃ

I shall deal with the commentaries' readings below.

What does this verse mean? Translators have had to choose between what seems to fit the original Pali and what would make sense in the context of the story. K. R. Norman has, as is his wont, stuck close to the original. His translation of *Thag* runs:

868 Truly it is a long time since a great seer, an ascetic, honoured by me, entered the great wood. Having heard your righteous verse, I shall abandon my numerous evils. (Norman, 1969:82)

The problem here is that in the story (of the *AS* – never mind the commentaries) it is not a long time since the Buddha entered the forest; yet to whom else could Aṅgulimāla be referring? Nor does it seem plausible that Aṅgulimāla had previously been honouring any ascetics at all. This could not even refer to the teacher invented by the commentaries, since he was in Taxila. A further problem is that the adverb *cirassaṃ* seems naturally to go with the verb nearest to it, which is *mahito*, 'honoured'. For *cirassa(ṃ)* the P.T.S. *Pali-English Dictionary* records only the meaning 'after a long time, at last'; for the corresponding Sanskrit *cirasya*, however, Monier-Williams also records the possible meaning 'for a long time', so this meaning might also apply in Pali.

The Ven. Nyanamoli (p. 195) translates the *AS*:

'Oh, at long last a sage revered by me,
This monk, has now appeared in the great forest:
Indeed I will for long renounce all evil,
Hearing your stanza showing the Dhamma.'

Translating *cirassā* in the third line as 'for long' gives a rather weak meaning and one wonders why Nyanamoli did not repeat 'at last'. Like Norman, he takes *cirassaṃ* in the first *pāda* not with the verb nearest to it but with the verb in the second *pāda*.

And like Norman he produces an implausible meaning, for his translation suggests that Aṅgulimāla had been honouring the Buddha ('this monk') before the moment at which he speaks the verse, but that is manifestly not the case.

Kurt Schmidt is clearly determined that his translation of the *AS* should make good sense. Ingeniously, he prints an asterisk and a gap between this and the previous verse, to indicate a complete break.[5] Then he translates:

> 'Einst trat zu mir im grossen Wald der Weise,
> Der hoch verehrte, (und ich sprach zu ihm:)
> Längst hätte ich das Böse aufgegeben,
> Wär' mir dein Wahrheitswort zuteil geworden.' (Schmidt, 1989:229)

I translate this into English:

> 'Long ago in the great forest the wise man, the greatly honoured, came to me (and I said to him): I would have given up wickedness long ago had your word of truth been bestowed upon me.'

Schmidt has seen the difficulty in the first line (*pāda*) and his solution is to put the first half of the verse in the present, long after the event, and then to supply 'and I said to him' in brackets. His translation of *pahāssaṃ* as a conditional 'I would have given up' is ingenious and grammatically possible, though it would not fit the *Thag* reading of the line, in which *cajissāmi* can only be a future. But Schmidt's interpretation depends on taking *cirassaṃ/cirassā* as 'long ago', twice, and the word never seems to have that meaning. This condemns his whole interpretation, for all its ingenuity. There are also lesser problems with it. If Aṅgulimāla is speaking long after his conversion, it would be

[5] In adopting this solution he is following the pioneer translation by Karl Eugen Neumann, *Die Reden Gotamo Buddhas aus der Mittleren Sammlung* (Munich 1900), II, 596.

very odd for him to refer to the Buddha as *samaṇo 'yaṃ*, 'this ascetic' – a fact that Schmidt tacitly recognises by omitting the words from his translation! Schmidt's translation also incurs the objection that I have made to the first two: that the adverb *cirassaṃ* seems naturally to go with *mahito*, but he takes it with *paccavādi/paccupādi*.

On this last point Miss Horner evidently agreed with me. Hers is the current P.T.S. translation of the MN. Here it runs:

'Long it is since a great sage was honoured by me, yet this recluse is penetrating the Great Grove. I will soon get rid of evil, hearing *dharma* in a verse of yours.' (Horner, 1957:286)

For the second *pāda*, Miss Horner has supplied 'yet' and has translated the main verb, which in either reading is an aorist, as a present; but neither point would vitiate her general interpretation. However, she has translated *cirassā* in the third *pāda* as 'soon', which suggests that she has supplied a negative which is not in the text. Her translation does make sense in the context and seems to me the best on offer, but it makes the verse appear somewhat disjointed. I hope to show that we can do better.

Let me now present the two commentaries on the verse. First the *Ps* (III, 33):

'Then the thief thought: "This is a great lion-roar, a great bellow. This bellow cannot be that of anyone else but Mahāmāyā's son Siddhattha, king of renunciates. Indeed (*vata*), I suppose the keen-eyed Buddha has seen me. The Blessed One has arrived to favour me." So he said *cirassam vata me* etc.. There *mahito* means honoured with offerings of the four requisites by gods and men. *Paccavādi* means he has come (*paṭipajji*) to this great forest after a long time to do me favour. *Pahassaṃ pāpaṃ* means I shall abandon (*pajahissāmi*) evil.'

There is a variant reading *paccupādi* for *paccavādi*. *Pahassaṃ* is here read with a central short *a* in accordance with general Pali phonetics. Other textual variants seem insignificant.

Dhammapāla in *Pad* (III, 57-8) expands on this without adding anything really new; but he of course has a different version of the third *pāda*.

'Aṅgulimāla had previously heard of the reputation of the Blessed One, which, fostered by his true qualities, had spread over the whole world like oil over water. For that reason, and because his knowledge had matured because all necessary conditions were present, he was delighted to realise that this was the Blessed One. He thought: "This is a great lion-roar, a great bellow. I think this can be that of no other renunciate, this is Gotama's roar. The great seer (*mahesi*), the Fully Enlightened, has indeed (*vata*) seen me. The Blessed One has arrived here to do me favour." So he spoke this verse. In it, *cirassaṃ vata* means after a long time indeed. *Me* means in order to favour me. *Mahito* means honoured with great honour by the world including the gods. He is *mahesi* because he wants (*esi*), seeks out, the great (*mahante*) qualities of the moral repertoire. *Mahāvanaṃ samaṇo paccupādi* means that he who has laid to rest (*samita*) all evil, the Blessed One, has come to this great forest. *So 'ham cajissāmi sahassa-pāpaṃ sutvāna* means that that person, namely I, heard your verse (*gāthā*) which was *dhamma-yuttaṃ*, provided with true teaching. He thought: "That person, namely I, on hearing that will abandon a thousand sins even after a long time, though associated with, practised, for a long time." And when he said, "Now most certainly I shall give it up," to show how he behaved and how he was favoured by the Blessed One the monks at the communal recitation put in the next two verses.'

The only textual variants here occur where Dhammapāla quotes our verse. In the second *pāda* the Burmese MS, as we have already noted above for the *AS*, reads *saccavādi*. In the third *pāda* the same Burmese source reads:

so 'haṃ carissāmi pahāya pāpaṃ 'So I shall live abandoning evil'.

The commentators leave no doubt that the *mahesi*, 'great seer', in the first *pāda* is the Buddha. It does seem to be true that *mahesi* in Pali always refers to the Buddha. Buddhaghosa agrees with Norman, Nyanamoli and Schmidt in taking the first *cirassaṃ* with the main verb at the end of the second *pāda*. Unlike any of the translators quoted, the commentators both detach *me* from *mahito* semantically; they interpret it as 'for my sake'. They do so because they see that it makes no sense for Aṅgulimāla to be saying at this stage that he has honoured the Buddha. But to detach *me* from *mahito* is linguistically awkward. Thus the commentators have a very clear perception of the problems with the first line, but cannot offer a plausible solution.

We shall return to the first line after considering the third. The Burmese variant just quoted both scans and makes good sense. Moreover, *carissāmi* might well underlie *cirassā* as a graphic corruption. Nevertheless, I do not think it likely to be the original reading: I prefer the *Thag* version of the line:

so 'haṃ cajissāmi sahassa-pāpaṃ 'So I shall abandon a thousand evils'.

This too scans, and *cajissāmi* could easily be corrupted into *carissāmi*. The decisive argument for this reading, however, is the thousand crimes. The *AS* (and *a fortiori* the *Thag*) makes no mention of Aṅgulimāla's being out for his thousandth finger when he encounters the Buddha; yet this was a detail which those who provided the episode with a background evidently felt the need to explain. In the *AS* story as it stands, he does not seem to require any particular number of fingers; his collection is open-ended. The idea that he needed a thousand must have arisen from an over-literal interpretation of this line.

The form *sahassa-pāpaṃ* does not present a problem, even though both in classical Sanskrit and in Pali the normal way of saying 'a thousand crimes' in a compound would be *pāpa-sahassaṃ*. *Sahassa-pāpaṃ* could be adequately explained as a *dvigu samāsa*: 'that which consists of a thousand crimes'. But the better explanation lies in pre-classical Sanskrit: Böhtlingk and

Roth quote, *s.v. sahasra, sahasrāśvena*, 'with a thousand horses', in the *Pañcaviṃśa Brāhmaṇa.*[6]

What of the first two *pādas*? We have already shown above that the version of the second line printed in the text of the *AS* in the P.T.S. edition has one syllable too many, whereas variant readings quoted in the footnotes do scan. We shall be able to decide which of those is to be preferred when we have further considered the first line, the root of the problem. No metrically correct version of that line is available. In his note on *Thag* 868, Norman tries to make it scan by deleting the *anusvāra* at the end of *cirassaṃ* and then claiming that there is a resolution of the fourth syllable of the line. This is technically just within the bounds of possibility, but resolution of the fourth syllable in a Pali *tuṭṭhubha* is exceedingly rare. Warder records no instance of it in his sample in *Pali Metre* (Warder, 1967:207-9). In Norman's own metrical tables for the *Thag*, this is the only example of it (Norman, 1969:xxxvii), and there is none in his corresponding table for the *Therīgāthā* (Norman, 1971:xx). The only corroborative evidence for such a resolution comes from resolution of the fourth syllable in a *jagatī*, which occurs at *Thag* 1142c, plus a possible instance in a corrupt-looking line at *Thag* 518a (Norman, 1969:xi).

Leaving scansion aside, the decisive objection to the first line as it stands lies in its meaning. As already explained, *mahesi* can only refer to the Buddha. So the natural meaning of the line as it stands would be 'after/for a long time I have honoured the great seer', namely the Buddha. But neither meaning of *cirassaṃ* fits the story: it is so implausible that this bloody brigand has been an admirer of the Buddha, waiting to meet him, that ancient commentators and modern translators alike have avoided this interpretation. There is the further incongruity that he then, according to the versions of the second line printed as the texts of the *AS* and *Thag*, refers to the Buddha much more casually, as

[6] I, 11, 17. Monier-Williams gives the form but omits the reference.

'this renunciate' or 'a renunciate'. He cannot refer to him at the same time as *mahesi* and as *samaṇo*.

Interpreters, in trying to avoid the line's 'natural' meaning, have also done some violence to the syntax of the stanza. I have already shown how some have taken the adverb *cirassaṃ* with the main verb at the end of the second line, rather than with *mahito*, the verb in the first line, thus going against what the word order would suggest. Here I must make a further syntactic point. The third *pāda* begins *so 'haṃ*. Such a use of the third person pronoun with the first (or second) person pronoun is always, I believe, anaphoric; it occurs when the first (or second) person has already been the topic. It is to bring out this anaphoric character that I rather clumsily translated *so 'haṃ* as 'that person, namely I' in my rendering of the *Pad* above. For this usage to be justified, I believe that *me* must be the logical subject of the first *pāda*. In other words, the commentators are wrong about *me*, and *me mahito* must go together and mean 'was honoured by me', i.e., 'I have honoured'. (The use of the genitive as agent with the past passive participle is common in Pali (von Hinüber, 1968:239-40, paras. 234-5); for its (more restricted) use in Sanskrit, see Pāṇini 2, 3, 67-8.)

So what is the solution? Having decided that the first line must be corrupt, I asked myself whom a man wearing a necklace of fingers might have been honouring for a long time. Textually it is easy to change *mahesi* into *maheso*. This change seems to resolve almost all our problems at one blow. Aṅgulimāla is revealed as a proto-Śaiva/Śākta, for Sanskrit *maheśa* (= Pali *maheso*) is a title of Śiva. There is no other evidence nearly as early as the Buddhist Canon for the sanguinary vows which led devotees of the Goddess to decorate themselves with parts of the human body often culled from living victims.[7] But the Buddhist evidence for such other extreme practices as the dog vow is similarly isolated. We simply possess very little evidence earlier than the Christian era (or indeed several centuries later) for any religious practices except those of Buddhists, Jains and orthoprax brahmins.

The mere change of the final vowel of the *pāda* is not enough to resolve the line's metrical problems; but we can now see in what direction a solution might lie. Aṅgulimāla is describing himself as a long-standing worshipper of 'the Great Lord', i.e., Śiva. His practice of collecting fingers for a necklace is thus sure to be the result of a vow, in which the worshipper tries to attain the iconic form of his god. The Pali word for a religious practice undertaken to fulfil a vow is *vata*. I cannot restore the *pāda* with absolute confidence, but for it to begin *ciraṃ vatā* would restore both metre and sense. I take *vatā* as a dative of purpose: 'for my votive practice', i.e., to fulfil a vow.[8] I presume that at a very early stage in the transmission of the text the 'vow' was lost by

[7] No one at the seminar questioned this identification. But I reported there, and should warn the reader, that it has been condemned by my colleague Professor Alexis Sanderson, who is a leading historian of Śaivism. I quote the most pertinent part of his letter to me: 'There is no evidence at all among Śaiva vratins [initiated Śaiva sectarian ascetics] at any time of "sanguinary vows ... victims". Devotees of Bhairava or Kālī were certainly enjoined to offer human sacrifices, but I know of no evidence, and you present none, that they ever decked themselves with the fingers or other body-parts of their victims. Initiates into these cults might observe a temporary or lifelong *kapālavratam/mahāvratam* in which they decked themselves with ornaments carved from human bones, used a human skull as a begging bowl, and wore a *yajñopavītam* [sacrificial thread] made from the twisted hair of a corpse. But all that is mortuary rather than sanguinary. The fact that the Goddess is sometimes decked with severed body-parts is irrelevant.' I am extremely grateful for his opinion, but remain willing to extrapolate from the very data he cites; see also below (p. 155). After all, we still are left with the question why someone should wear a necklace of fingers.

[8] For the form see Geiger and Norman, 1994:19, para.27.2. In the circulated version of this chapter I suggested in the body of the text that *vatā* was ablative, meaning 'because of a vow', and gave the dative as an alternative in a footnote. I am grateful to Alexis Sanderson for pointing out to me that *vatā* never means 'vow', but 'vowed practice', so that the ablative is extremely unlikely.

those who had no idea about such practices; they turned it into the otiose particle *vata*, 'indeed'.

What about the second *pāda*? I prefer the Burmese *mahāvanaṃ pāpuṇi saccavādi*. It makes excellent sense for Aṅgulimāla here to address the Buddha as 'speaker of truth', for it is precisely the – paradoxical – truth he has just uttered that has converted the brigand and led to the resolution expressed in the next line. That the author of the prose *AS* read *saccavādi* is also rendered likely by the fact that in the prose, after the Buddha has said that he has stopped, Aṅgulimāla says to himself, 'These renunciates of the Sakyan are truthful and keep their word (*saccavādino saccapaṭiññā*)' (p. 99).[9] *Saccavādi* could have been corrupted, by confusion of the letters *s* and *p*, into *paccavādi*, a form which does not occur elsewhere but was interpreted as a verb meaning 'arrived'. In the *Thag* text, and in Sinhala MSS and the Siamese printed edition of the *AS*, this is read as *paccupādi*; this too would be a unique form. As Norman says in his note on *Thag* 868, this could be a mistake for *paccapādi*, but it is unclear why such a mistaken writing of a non-existent form should have occurred. Since *pāpuṇi* and *paccavādi/paccupādi* then seemed to have the same meaning, the former may have been interpreted as a gloss on the latter and removed from the text, and *samaṇo* introduced as repair work, the verb having been interpreted as third person.

Which person in fact is *pāpuṇi*? As written, it is ambiguous between the second and third persons singular. But a third possibility must be kept in mind: that it stands for the first person singular, *pāpuṇiṃ*, with loss of *anusvāra* (and presumably nasalised pronunciation of the *i*) by a common metrical license. Whoever wrote *samaṇo* interpreted the verb as third person; but this seems to me to yield a clearly inferior meaning in the dialogue. For me the choice lies between taking it as second person, anticipating *tava* in the fourth line, and taking it as first

[9] This was pointed out to me by Dr Sally Mellick Cutler.

person. The latter would give the smoothest construction with *so 'haṃ*: 'I came to the great forest, O speaker of truth, and now I ....' However, it seems likely that Aṅgulimāla would have been living in the forest already and that it was the Buddha's arrival there which required mention. I find the arguments rather equally weighted but on balance I would take the verb as second person. One textual tradition apparently agreed with me in this detail: the Siamese variant of the *AS* text has *samaṇa* in the vocative.[10] I take this to be an intermediate stage in the text on the way to *samaṇo*, a stage at which it was somehow remembered that the verb should be in the second person. If *pāpuṇi* is indeed second person, *saccavādi* is better translated as a nominative rather than a vocative, as this gives it more weight.

To sum up, I read and translate as follows:

ciraṃ vatā me mahito mah eso *mahāvanaṃ pāpuṇi saccavādī*
so 'haṃ cajissāmi sahassapāpaṃ *sutvāna gāthaṃ tava dhammayuttaṃ*

'For a long time to fulfil a vow I have been honouring Śiva. You have arrived in the forest, speaking truth. So I shall give up my thousand crimes, for I have heard your verse, which teaches what is right.'

It only remains to point out that the first three verses would make sense as a summary account of Aṅgulimāla's conversion without positing the miraculous element that he was running fast but could not catch the walking Buddha. That piece of the story could have arisen as a mere over-interpretation of the word play.

* * *

[10] For this variant to scan, the final syllable of *samaṇa* would have to be lengthened. As it is a vocative and might be followed by a short pause, this seems to me a not impossible licence.

How does this discovery fit into the history of Indian religion? There is only fragmentary evidence for the cluster of religious practices known as *tantra* before the seventh century A.D., more than a thousand years after our text. But Aṅgulimāla's necklace of fingers would not be the only evidence for such practices to be found in the Pali Canon.

Tantra rests on the idea, which permeates the local traditions of South and Southeast Asia, that a worshipper can somehow identify with his god in a literal sense. The most widespread form in which such identification is practised is possession: the god (male or female) is thought to enter, control and become manifest in the body of the worshipper (male or female). This idea underlies most of the sophisticated theology, both tantric and devotional, of Indian theism. The tantric, no less than the village medium, normally acts out this identification by adopting the deity's iconic appearance, wearing his or her accoutrements. In the *Pāśupata Sūtras*[11] the Śaivite ascetic of the *pāśupata* sect is enjoined (*sūtra* 1, 6) to be *liṅgadhārī*, i.e., wear the god's emblems, just as we can still see Śaivite village priests rubbing sacred ash over themselves and carrying the god's weapons (Gombrich & Obeyesekere, 1988: figures 6, 9). Thus attired, the worshipper also emulates the god's behaviour, though the extent to which this emulation is carried out literally or only in the imagination varies enormously.

Tantra also depends on the idea that one can draw power from impurity. The brahminical norms of purity are themselves partly based on the idea that the world is full of dangerous forces, whether these are embodied in corpses and in bodily secretions such as blood, semen and excreta or personified as spirits who enjoy such impure substances. To preserve purity is at the same time a matter of avoiding impure substances and keeping the personified forces of darkness at bay. Purity is a code for social

[11] Ed. R. Ananthakṛishna Sastri, *Trivandrum Sanskrit Series* CXLIII, Trivandrum 1940.

and religious status; but since it excludes powerful forces it is also a kind of self-imposed impotence. The tantric tries to harness the forces of impurity. If he blunders, they may destroy him; but if he knows the right technique he may master them. The black magician who runs the risk of being destroyed by the forces with which he dabbles is a figure probably familiar the world over. What is distinctive to the Indian tradition is the ways in which the magician seeks his mastery by identifying himself with the spirit who personifies the power he wishes to use.

When those practices become theologised under the influence of brahminical philosophy, especially the doctrine of non-dualism, mastery of the forces of darkness comes to be conceptualised as transcendence of the duality between purity and impurity, between good and evil. This transcendence is essential when tantra becomes a path to salvation. At that stage the divinity with whom one identifies likewise transcends all mundane dualities. But when tantra is used for worldly power, its origin in the dark side of the purity/impurity divide remains evident, and so does the antinomian character of its deities. These deities not only demand blood sacrifice; they frequent the areas outside ordered social life: the jungle, and in extreme cases the cemetery or charnel ground. Ideally the Hindu corpse is in most cases burnt, but poor people could often not afford the necessary firewood, so that corpses were often just abandoned half burnt or even not burnt at all. The cemetery was thus a terrifying place, the haunt of powerful ghouls and vampires.

Antinomian practices in India have never been so systematised that they could all be classified under sects worshipping one or other of the gods known to us from brahminical literature. We quoted above records in the Pali Canon of antinomian practices which tried to derive power and/or salvation precisely from transgressing the norms of the wider, brahmin-dominated society. The naked ascetic in the *Pāṭika Sutta* who lives on meat and strong drink is evidently such an antinomian; classical tantrics ritually consume such 'impure' foods. Adopting the lifestyles of dogs and cows is similarly antinomian behaviour, though not part of the classical tantric complex.

Tantric practices and ideas spread into every classical Indian religious tradition in the mediaeval period; but the deities whom most early tantrics worshipped were forms of Śiva and the Goddess (Devī), Śiva's power personified. The Goddess also has a mythology of her own, and whether a sect is to be classified as Śaiva or Śākta depends largely on whether she is seen primarily as Śiva's consort or more as powerful in her own right. Historically the Śaiva/Śākta religious complex can be treated as one, containing many nuances and many related traditions of practice and ideology.

Śiva is known under the name of Rudra in the *Ṛg Veda*, and is associated with the darker side of life, a menacing outsider. He has many roles and many names: to what extent those constitute a single coherent entity or an amalgam of traditions from different times, places and contexts is not a question we can here discuss.

There is very little evidence about the Goddess in Vedic texts. In later times the commonest name which she bears in her terrific form is Kālī, 'the black one'. Correspondingly, Śiva can bear the name Mahākāla, 'the great black one'. This is ambiguous, as *kāla* also means 'time' and is a name for death; thus Mahākāla can also mean 'Great Death'. The close association with death can spill over to Kālī, who typically frequents cemeteries and decorates herself with corpses.

For a detailed description of how Kālī is to be visualised we turn to the *Kālī Tantra*. This is a relatively modern text, almost certainly dating from the present millennium, which is extremely popular with Śāktas in eastern India.[12] It contains the *dhyāna* of the goddess, i.e., the prescription for how she is to be visualised. Human parts figure several times in this description: she is decorated with a garland of skulls (*muṇḍamālāvibhūṣitām*); of her four hands, the upper left one holds a newly severed head

[12] Sanjukta Gupta, personal communication.

(*sadyaśchinnaśiraḥ* ... *vāmordhva* ... *karāmbujām*); she is smeared with the blood dripping from the line of skulls strung round her neck (*kaṇṭhāvasakta-muṇḍālīgaladrudhiracarcitām*); fearsome with a pair of corpses used as her earrings (*karṇāvataṃsatānītaśavayugmabhayānakām*) (these are probably infants' corpses); and has a girdle of hands collected from corpses (*śavānāṃ karasaṃghātaiḥ kṛtakāñcīm*).[13]

To adduce so modern a description of Kālī may seem out of place here. But the Pali Canon contains an account of Kālī which, though tantalisingly brief, affords strong grounds for thinking that she was not very differently visualised well over two thousand years ago.

In the *Thera-gāthā* we find a pair of stanzas, 151-2, attributed to a monk with the *prima facie* surprising name of Mahākāla:

Kālī itthī brahatī dhaṅkarūpā
satthiṃ ca bhetvā aparaṃ ca satthiṃ
bāhaṃ ca bhetvā aparaṃ ca bāhaṃ
sīsaṃ ca bhetvā dadhithālikaṃ va
esā nisinnā abhisandahitvā.

Yo ve avidvā upadhiṃ karoti
punappunaṃ dukkham upeti mando.
Tasmā pajānaṃ upadhiṃ na kayirā
Māhaṃ puna bhinnasiro sayissan ti.

K. R. Norman translates (Norman, 1969:20):

'151. The large swarthy woman, like a crow, having broken a thigh-bone and then another, having broken an arm and then another, having broken a skull like a curds-bowl, is seated having heaped them together.

[13] *Kālītantra* ed. and pub. Khemarāja Śrīkṛṣṇadāsa, Bombay saṃvat 2029 (1972 AD.), p. 35.

152. The fool who being ignorant makes a basis for rebirth comes to pain again and again. Therefore one who knows should not make a basis for rebirth. May I never lie again with my skull broken.'

For the last word of the first stanza there are variant readings: *abhisaddahitvā* and *abhinnahitvā*. I emend to *abhisannahitvā*. For *abhi-sam-nah* Monier-Williams' *Sanskrit-English Dictionary* gives the meanings 'to bind or string together' and 'to arm oneself against'; under the past passive participle, *abhisaṃnaddha*, it gives 'armed'. Thus I take *abhisaṃnahitvā* to mean 'stringing together and wearing as an accoutrement'.

The commentary, *Pad* II, 27, has (in my view) no idea what is going on.[14] It says that Mahākāla was a merchant, a caravan leader, who was converted by hearing the Buddha preach. He took up practising in a cemetery (*sosānikaṅgaṃ adhiṭṭhāya susāne vasati*), one of the recognised ascetic practices (*dhutaṅga*) of Buddhist monks. It continues:

'Then one day a woman called Kāḷī, a corpse-burner, took a recent corpse, broke off both its thighs and arms, broke the skull like a pot of yoghurt, put all its parts together and set it in a suitable place for the elder to see, so that he could meditate on it. Then she sat down to one side. The elder saw it, and to admonish himself said: ....' (Here follow the two verses.)

My interpretation of the verses is as follows. Mahākāla must, like Aṅgulimāla, be a Śaiva/Śākta converted to Buddhism. Mahākāla is the name he assumed in order to identify with Śiva. He used to visit cemeteries in order to visualise Kālī there, and the first verse describes such a visualisation. Kālī in the verse is the name, not just a description, and *itthī* does not mean that she is a human woman – it can be applied to goddesses (or demonesses)

[14] The same story recurs at *Dhammapada-atthakathā* I, 66-74.

as well.[15] The meditator sees her take limbs from corpses and garland herself with them. She takes a skull which is dripping with brains (as the commentary correctly explains); the mention of yoghurt may also imply that she is using the skull as a food-bowl, and consequently that that was what her worshipper was meant to do,[16] as we know to have been done later by the Śaiva Kāpālika sect (Lorenzen, 1991:5). The word *esā*, 'here', shows that Mahākāla can see her sitting right in front of him. While or after doing this visualisation he realises (in the second verse) that as soon as he dies his own corpse may be similarly dismembered and his skull put to such use.

I need hardly stress how unconvincing is the commentary's Buddhist rationalisation of the episode. A monk who goes to a cemetery to meditate on corpses will find plenty and does not need the services of an employee to arrange a pile of limbs for him, nor is it Buddhist practice to dismember or otherwise interfere with corpses.

* * *

This is such a choice piece of evidence that I do not think that the paucity of other references to Śiva and Kālī in the Pali Canon need worry us. But let me collect those other references here. A god Śiva (*Sivo devaputto*) is mentioned without elaboration in the *Saṃyutta Nikāya* (I, 56-7). In the list of wrong ways for an ascetic to make a living (DN I, 9), there occurs a list of knowledges (*vijjā*) of the kind which today might be called

[15] Professor Sanderson writes: '*Itthī* in my opinion proves conclusively that the *Theragāthā* is speaking of a human being. The goddess would never be referred to as *strī* in Sanskrit.' Here, however, I feel sure of my ground. Professor Sanderson is referring to texts composed by and for Kālī-worshippers. Buddhists traditionally have a very different and far less respectful attitude to her (see Gombrich & Obeyesekere, 1988: chapter 4). I have indeed asked Sinhala informants whether it would jar on them to call Kālī a 'woman' (Sinhala: *istrī*) and they were definite that it would not. The use of the term *naradeva* to denote a male god in Pali (SN I, 5; SN I, 200) seems to provide a parallel.

[16] I owe this suggestion to Sanjukta Gupta. Professor Sanderson finds it implausible.

'occult'. In this list occurs *siva-vijjā*. The commentary (DA I, 93) gives two explanations: 'The knowledge of how to pacify [*santi-karaṇa*, a term for white magic] when one has been living in a cemetery. They also say it is knowledge of the cries of jackals.' There are indeed sciences of prognostication from the cries and other behaviour of fauna. But the former explanation seems more likely to be correct, for two reasons. Firstly, 'jackal' is *sivā*, feminine, not *siva*. Secondly, the next item in the list is *bhūta-vijjā*, a well-known term for necromancy, i.e. dealing with ghosts or ghouls.

Another Sanskrit name of Śiva is Īśāna; this name is particularly used in ritual contexts where he is the presiding deity of the north-eastern direction. In the *Tevijja Sutta* the Buddha ridicules brahmins who hope to go to join Brahmā in heaven when they die by invoking a list of gods, and Īsāna is among the gods listed whom it is fatuous to invoke (DN I, 244). Īsāna is also mentioned as a king of the gods (*devarāja*) at SN I, 219; this text, the *Dhajagga Sutta*, is one of those often recited for apotropaic purposes (*paritta*).

Though Maheśa is a common name for Śiva in Sanskrit texts from the *Mahābhārata* onwards, it has not been found so far in the Pali Canon. But I suspect that it has been lurking there all along. Maheśa literally means 'great lord' and thus looks as if it could be applied to any god, but in Hindu practice it seems always to be a title or epithet of Śiva. In the Canon gods are sometimes referred to as *mahesakkha* and *appesakkha*, traditionally interpreted as meaning 'of great power' and 'of little power'. I suggest that *mahesakkha* comes from Sanskrit *maheśākhya* (*mahā-īśa-ākhya*), meaning 'called Maheśa', and that the term originated in a context where it referred to Śiva; it was then misunderstood and generalised. (*Appesakkha* would be an analogical formation.)

There is indisputable evidence for Kālī. We saw above (p. 79) that in the *Māra-tajjaniya Sutta* (*sutta* 50), Mahā Moggallāna tells Māra that he, Māra, is (or was) the son of Kālī, who in a former age, during the lifetime of the Buddha Kakusandha, was the sister of a Māra called Dūsi (MN I, 333). Calling Kālī the sister of Māra sounds suspiciously like a satirical allusion to her relationship with Mahākāla. Another reference too sounds satirical: a particularly quarrelsome and abusive nun was called Caṇḍakālī (Vin IV, 230, 276-7, 293, 309, 331, 333). Caṇḍī, 'ferocious' has always been an epithet of Kālī. Here it looks as if a woman renowned for her bad temper acquired Caṇḍakālī as a nickname.

* * *

Aṅgulimāla collected his fingers from living victims, not corpses. This is not implausible. In Indian tradition, Kālī is the patron saint of robbers, and their custom of making blood sacrifices to her, even from human victims, has survived until modern times. In Buddhaghosa's *Visuddhi-magga* (IX, para.41), bandits come upon some monks in a forest and say that they need to kill one of them to use the blood from his throat as an offering (*bali*). Unfortunately the text does not specify the deity. Though this text dates from the beginning of the fifth century A.D., we know that Buddhaghosa usually, if not always, uses much older material. This is not a story but an illustration of an ethical dilemma and would lose its point if such a situation never occurred in real life.

In fact we know that it did occur in real life. When the Chinese pilgrim Hiuen Tsiang was going down the Ganges from Ayodhyā, he and his party were captured by river pirates. The pirates decided to sacrifice the Chinese monk to Durgā and he was only saved by a providential storm, which so scared the pirates that they converted to Buddhism (Watters, 1904:360). Thus more than a thousand years later, in the same part of India, a Buddhist monk virtually recapitulated the Buddha's experience with Aṅgulimāla. If Hiuen Tsiang had known what that experience of the Buddha's really was, we would have a right to be suspicious that the coincidence was a hagiographic fabrication;

but he did not know. So his experience forms the perfect pendent to our story.

I think we can safely say that for about a thousand years Buddhism in India was a religion which could be characterised as antithetical to tantra, or at least to Śaiva/Śākta tantra, which was the tantric religion par excellence. Firstly, Buddhism cultivated self-control in general, and in particular meditative states in which self-awareness is gradually enhanced to the point of total self-knowledge. In a possessed person, normal self-control and self-awareness are totally suppressed. The fact that in traditional Sinhala society possession is seen as antithetical to Buddhist values is clearly shown by the fact that the institutionalised spirit cults which depend on a medium (*kapuvā*) do not operate on a *poya* day, the weekly day of enhanced Buddhist observance. Secondly, Buddhism *per se*, being unconcerned with worldly matters, did not recognise brahminical concepts of impurity. Thus in Sinhala Buddhism a woman who is menstruating may not, for example, attend a spirit shrine, but her condition does not affect her attendance at a Buddhist temple or her participation in any act of Buddhist piety. Thirdly, Buddhism was never antinomian and under no circumstances could normal morality be transcended. To this the whole of Sinhala Buddhism bears witness: the whole cosmos is organised on ethical principles, and a god who will accede to an unethical request is *ipso facto* a kind of demon (*yakṣa*).

There is perhaps a certain irony in the fact that somewhere around the time when Hiuen Tsiang was under threat of being made a sacrificial victim – we cannot specify the date closer than by a couple of centuries – Buddhism was massively invaded by tantra, and the Vajrayāna tradition was born. Both in depending on the practitioner's identification with gods/demons, a sophisticated ideologisation of possession, and in drawing power from impurity, Buddhist tantra is paradoxical Buddhism and has turned the tradition on its head in a way which deserves the label of syncretism. But it has been recolonised by Buddhist ethics: its purposes are never immoral, but the allegorical dramas enacted in

Buddhist ritual and visualised by its practitioners always witness the triumph of good over evil, and are interpreted as leading to Enlightenment. In other words, what makes the Vajrayāna Buddhist is its ethics. Figuratively we may say that the Buddha converted not only Aṅgulimāla but Aṅgulimāla's entire religion.

Bibliography of Secondary Sources

Alsdorf, Ludwig, 1968: *Die Āryā-Strophen des Pali-Kanons*, Akademie der Wissenschaften und Literatur, Mainz.

Brough, John, 1953: *The early Brahmanical system of Gotra and Pravara*, Cambridge.

Carter, John Ross, 1978: *Dhamma, Western Academic and Sinhalese Buddhist Interpretations, A Study of a Religious Concept*, Tokyo.

Causton, Richard, 1988: *Nichiren Shōshū Buddhism: An Introduction*, London.

Collins, Steven, 1982: *Selfless Persons*, Cambridge.

Falk, Harry, 1993: *Schrift in alten Indien: ein Forschungsbericht mit Anmerkungen*, Tübingen.

Fergusson, James, 1873: *Tree and Serpent Worship*, 2nd ed., London.

Fischer, Eberhard and Jain, Jyotindra, 1974: *Kunst und Religion in Indien: 2500 Jahre Jainismus*, Zurich.

Frauwallner, Erich, 1956: *The Earliest Vinaya and the Beginnings of Buddhist Literature, Serie Orientale Roma VIII*, Is.M.E.O., Rome.

Frauwallner, Erich, 1973: *History of Indian Philosophy*, vol.1, tr. V.M. Bedekar, Delhi.

Geiger, Wilhelm 1994: *A Pāli Grammar*, tr. Batakrishna Ghosh, revised & ed. K. R. Norman, Pali Text Society, Oxford.

Geiger, Magdalene and Wilhelm, 1920: *Pāli DHAMMA, vornehmlich in der kanonischen Literatur, Abhandlungen der Bayerischen Akademie, Philosophisch-philologische und historische Klasse* 31,1, Munich.

Gelblum, Tuvia, 1970: 'Sāṃkhya and Sartre', *Journal of Indian Philosophy* 1, pp.75-82.

Gethin, R. M. L., 1992: *The Buddhist Path to Awakening*, Leiden.

Gombrich, Richard, 1971: *Precept and Practice*, Oxford.

Gombrich, Richard, 1975: 'Ancient Indian Cosmology', *Ancient Cosmologies,* ed. Carmen Blacker and Michael Loewe, London, pp.110-142.

Gombrich, Richard, 1980: 'The significance of former Buddhas in Theravādin tradition', *Buddhist Studies in Honour of Walpola Rahula*, ed. S. Balasooriya et al., London, pp.62-72.

Gombrich, Richard, 1988a: 'The History of Early Buddhism: Major Advances since 1950', *Indological Studies in South Asian Bibliography – a Conference, 1986*, National Library, Calcutta, pp.12-30.

Gombrich, Richard, 1988b: *Theravāda Buddhism: A Social History from Ancient Benares to Modern Colombo*, London; corrected edition 1994.

Gombrich, Richard and Obeyesekere, Gananath, 1988: *Buddhism Transformed*, Princeton.

Gombrich, Richard, 1990: 'Recovering the Buddha's Message', *The Buddhist Forum: Seminar papers 1987-1988*, ed. T. Skorupski, SOAS, London, pp.5-23; reprinted in *Earliest Buddhism and Madhyamaka*, ed. D. Ruegg and L. Schmithausen, Leiden.

Gombrich, Richard, 1992a: 'Dating the Buddha: A Red Herring Revealed', *The Dating of the Historical Buddha Part 2*, ed. Heinz Bechert, Göttingen, pp.237-259.

Gombrich, Richard, 1992b: 'The Buddha's Book of Genesis?', *Indo-Iranian Journal* 35, pp.159-178.

Gombrich, Richard, 1992c: 'Why six former Buddhas?', *The Journal of Oriental Research*, The Kuppuswami Sastri Research Institute, Madras, pp.326-330.

Gombrich, Richard, 1992d: 'A momentous effect of translation: The 'vehicles' of Buddhism.' *Apodosis: Essays presented to Dr.W.W. Cruickshank to mark his 80th birthday*, St.Paul's School, London, pp.34-46.

Gombrich, Richard, 1993a: 'Buddhist prediction: how open is the future?'. Darwin College Lecture printed in *Predicting the Future*, Cambridge, ed. Leo Howe and Alan Wain, pp.144-168.

Gombrich, Richard, 1993b: 'Understanding early Buddhist Terminology in its Context', *Pali Daejangkang Urimal Olmgim Nonmon Moum II / 'A Korean Translation of Pali Tripitaka Vol. II'*, pp.74-101.

Gombrich, Richard, 1994a: 'What is Pali?', *A Pali Grammar*, W.Geiger, tr. B.Ghosh, rev. & ed. K. R. Norman, Pali Text Society, pp.xxiii-xxix.

Gombrich, Richard, 1994b: 'The Buddha and the Jains: A Reply to Professor Bronkhorst', *Asiatische Studien* XLVIII 4, pp.1069-1096.

Gomez, L.O., 1976: 'Proto-Mādhyamika in the Pali Canon', *Philosophy East and West* xxvi, 2, pp.137-165.

Gupta, Sanjukta, 1991: 'The Buddha Avatāra', *Studies in Buddhism and culture in honour of Professor Dr. Egaku Mayeda on his sixty-fifth birthday*. The Editorial Committee of the Felicitation Volume for Professor Dr. Egaku Mayeda, Tokyo, pp.176-7.

Hamilton, S.B., 1993: Oxford D.Phil thesis: *The Constitution of the Human Being According to Early Buddhism.* To appear as *Identity and Experience: the Constitution of the Human Being according to Early Buddhism*, London, 1995.

Hara, Minoru, 1994: 'Transfer of Merit in Hindu Literature and Religion', *The Memoirs of the Toyo Bunko* 52, pp.103-135.

von Hinüber, Oskar, 1968: *Studien zur Kasussyntax des Pāli, besonders des Vinayapiṭaka*, Munich.

Härtel, Herbert, 1993: *Excavations at Sonkh*, Berlin.

von Hinüber, Oskar, 1978: '*Gotrabhū*: Die sprachliche Vorgeschichte eines philosophischen Terminus', *ZDMG* 128, pp.326-332.

Horner, I. B. (tr.), 1957: *The Middle Length Sayings* II, Pali Text Society, London.

Johnson, W.J., 1990: *The Problem of Bondage in Selected Early Jaina Texts*, D.Phil. thesis, Oxford.

Lamotte, Étienne, 1935-6: 'Le traité de l'acte de Vasubandhu Karmasiddhiprakaraṇa', *Mélanges chinois et bouddhiques* 4, pp.151-206.

de La Vallée Poussin, Louis, 1927: *La morale bouddhique*, Paris.

de La Vallée Poussin, Louis, 1936-7: 'Musīla et Nārada: Le Chemin de Nirvāṇa', *Mélanges chinois et bouddhiques* V, pp.189-222.

Lloyd, G. E. R., 1990: *Demystifying Mentalities*, Cambridge.

Lorenzen, David N., 1991: *The Kāpālikas and Kālāmukhas*, 2nd. ed. Delhi.

Malalasekera, G. P., 1937: *Dictionary of Pāli Proper Names*, London.

Miller, Barbara Stoler, 1979: 'On Cultivating the Immeasurable Change of Heart: the Buddhist Brahma-Vihāra Formula', *Journal of Indian Philosophy* 7, pp.209-221.

Mumford, Stan Royal, 1989: *Himalayan Dialogue: Tibetan Lamas and Gurung Shamans in Nepal*, Madison.

Norman, K. R. (tr.), 1969: *The Elders' Verses* I, Pali Text Society, Oxford.

Norman, K. R. (tr.), 1971: *The Elders' Verses* II, Pali Text Society, Oxford.

Norman, K. R., 1981: 'A note on *Attā* in the *Alagaddūpama Sutta*', *Studies in Indian Philosophy: A Memorial Volume in Honour of Pandit Sukhlaji Sanghvi*, *LD series* 84, Ahmedabad.

Norman, K. R., 1983: *Pāli Literature*, Wiesbaden.

Nyanamoli, Ven. Thera, ed. Phra Khantipalo, no date: *A Treasury of the Buddha's Discourses from the Majjhima-nikāya (Middle Collection)* vol.1, [Wat Buddha-Dhamma, Wisemans Ferry, N.S.W., Australia].

Oldenberg, Hermann, 1923: *Die Lehre der Upanishaden und die Anfänge des Buddhismus*, 2nd ed, Göttingen.

Popper, Karl R., 1952: *The Open Society and its Enemies*, 2nd (revised) ed., 2 vols., London.

Popper, Karl R., 1960: *The Poverty of Historicism*, 2nd ed., London.

Popper, Karl R., 1972: 'On the Theory of the Objective Mind', *Objective Knowledge: An Evolutionary Approach*, Oxford, pp.53-190.

Popper, Karl R., 1974: *Conjectures and Refutations*, 5th ed., London.

Prasad, H. K., 1960: 'The Nāga-Cult in Bihar', *Journal of the Bihar Research Society* 46, pp.129-134.

Rhys Davids, T. W. (tr.), 1899: *Dialogues of the Buddha* I, Pali Text Society, London.

Rhys Davids, T. W., 1903: *Buddhist India*, London.

Rhys Davids, T. W. and C. A. F. (tr.), 1910: *Dialogues of the Buddha* II, Pali Text Society, London.

Ruegg, D. Seyfort, 1974: 'Pali *gotta/gotra* and the term *gotrabhū* in Pali and Sanskrit', *Buddhist Studies in Honour of I.B.Horner*, ed. Lance Cousins et al., Dordrecht, pp.199-210.

Ruegg, David Seyfort, 1989: *Buddha-nature, Mind and the Problem of Gradualism in a Comparative Perspective: On the Transmission and Reception of Buddhism in India and Tibet*, London.

Samuel, Geoffrey, 1993: *Civilized Shamans*, Washington and London.

Schmidt, Kurt (tr.), 1989: *Buddhas Reden*, 2nd.ed. Leimen.

Smith, Peter and Jones, O.R., 1986: *The Philosophy of Mind: An Introduction*, Cambridge.

Spiro, Melford, 1970: *Buddhism and Society: A Great Tradition and its Burmese Vicissitudes*, New York.

Stargardt, Janice, 1995: 'The Oldest Known Pali Texts, 5th-6th century; Results of the Cambridge Symposium on the Pyu Golden Pali Text from Śrī Kṣetra, 18-19 April 1995', *Journal of the Pali Text Society*, vol. XXI, pp.199-214.

Takasaki, Jikido, 1987: *An Introduction to Buddhism*, trans. Rolf W. Giebel, Tokyo.

Takasaki, Jikido, 1992: 'On *Gotrabhū*', *Wiener Zeitschrift für die Kunde Südasiens XXXVI/Supplementband*, pp.251-9.

Rahula, Walpola, 1956: *History of Buddhism in Ceylon*, Colombo.

Warder, A. K., 1967: *Pali Metre*, Pali Text Society, London.

Watters, Thomas, 1904: *On Yuan Chwang's Travels in India 629-645 A.D.*, Royal Asiatic Society, London.

Williams, Paul M., 1990: *Mahāyāna Buddhism: the Doctrinal Foundations*, London.

Wilson, Bryan and Dobbelaere, Karel, 1994: *A Time to Chant: The Sōka Gakkai Buddhists in Britain*, Oxford.

Woodward, F. L. (tr.), 1932: *The Book of the Gradual Sayings* I, Pali Text Society, London.

Woodward, F. L. (tr.), 1933: *The Book of the Gradual Sayings* II, Pali Text Society, London.

Zürcher, E., 1959: *The Buddhist Conquest of China*, Leiden.

General Index

Index of Texts Cited